COLLEGE SUCCESS YOUR WAY:

What Your Professors Won't Tell You and Your Friends Don't Know

Your Guide to the Easiest Path to Success in College and Beyond

CRYSTAL ◆ JONAS

Tap Your Genius, Inc.,
Manitou Springs, Colorado

Go to CollegeLifeSite.com for more Success Programs and Products

Published by
Tap Your Genius, Inc.
Manitou Springs, CO
Crystal@CrystalJonas.com
www.crystaljonas.com

Unattributed quotations are by Crystal Jonas

Printed in the United States of America

Print Version:
ISBN: 9780976934455

Library of Congress Control Number: 2006905397

Text editing by Jaclyn Jonas Castro
Cover and text design by Janet Bergin, empoweryourawesomeness.com

My lawyer makes me say this: The purpose of this book is to educate and entertain. This book does not promise that anyone following the ideas, tips, suggestions, or strategies will successfully complete college. The author, publisher, and distributors shall have neither liability nor responsibility to anyone with respect to any loss or damage caused, or alleged to be caused, directly or indirectly by the information contained in this book.

ACKNOWLEDGEMENTS

I am deeply grateful to my family for their love and support.

To the world's greatest kids, Tyler, Jaclyn, and Cameron: You are all three so fun, funny, talented and smart. Being your Mom is my great privilege and pleasure.

I love you.

Keynotes and Seminars for College Students of All Ages

Our most popular topics include:

1) "Succeed in College: What Your Professors Won't Tell You and Your Friends Don't Know"
- Professors' pet peeves to avoid at all cost
- The simple secrets of smart students
- Time & self-management; better results, less effort
- Keys to getting a head start on your dream job

2) "How to Lead So Others Will Follow"
- Image makers and breakers every leader should know
- Essential ingredients of dynamic leadership
- Communication skills that enhance teamwork
- How to inspire others to be who they are at their best

3) "Jump-start Your Career"
- The paved path to professional progress starts here
- How to get high-viz, no pressure job interviews
- How your professors can help you land your dream job
- 7 skills that will get you hired and promoted quickly

Special Bonus

Crystal delivers to colleges and corporations over 100 paid presentations a year, to invite her to speak to your college students, faculty or staff, contact: (719) 291-0366 or E-mail: Crystal@CrystalJonas.com

CONTENTS

CHAPTER 1
JUMP-START YOUR COLLEGE SUCCESS   1

CHAPTER 2
PET PEEVES THAT DRIVE PROFESSORS UP THE WALL   11

CHAPTER 3
HOW TO GET BETTER GRADES WITH LESS EFFORT   21

CHAPTER 4
DISCOVER THE SIMPLE SECRETS OF SMART STUDENTS   31

CHAPTER 5
MIND TRICKS THAT MAKE LEARNING A PIECE OF CAKE   45

CHAPTER 6
**THINK OUTSIDE THE BOOKS: NONTRADITIONAL
SOLUTIONS FOR NONTRADITIONAL STUDENTS**   53

CHAPTER 7
LAUNCH A GREAT CAREER WHILE STILL IN SCHOOL   61

CHAPTER 8
TAKE THE FAST TRACK TO PROFESSIONAL SUCCESS   73

CHAPTER 9
LIVING AN EXTRAORDINARY LIFE   81

SNAPSHOTS FROM THE JOURNEY   94

ABOUT THE AUTHOR   118

**KEYNOTES AND SEMINARS FOR COLLEGE
STUDENTS OF ALL AGES**   119

INDEX   120

To hire Crystal to speak at your College contact:
Crystal Jonas
Crystal@CrystalJonas.com
719-291-0366

Your guide for how to succeed in college and beyond and still have time for a life

Think of this guide as your road map for moving through your college career and into a rewarding professional career with ease and maximum enjoyment.

I wrote this book especially for every hardworking student who wants to do well in college and doesn't want to take all four years to figure out how to do that.

Throughout this book, you'll encounter signs that will help you quickly know how to navigate the exciting (and sometimes bumpy!) road of higher education.

With experience as a college professor, academic advisor, and peak performance expert, I'll give you the insider's guide to making college a huge success.

I've shown students from all over the world how to unlock their natural power to achieve amazing results in their lives, from how to ace academics, to simple ways to fit in fast, to succeeding in "the real world."

I welcome your ideas and success stories. Let me know how you've used these practical and powerful tips in your own life.

All the best to you.

Crystal Jonas
Manitou Springs

JUMP-START YOUR COLLEGE SUCCESS

DISCOVER:

- The bad habit that can lower any grade

- A tiny transgression that's more damaging than you think

- What your professors will never tell you about class participation

- The surprising truth about extra credit

- How your professors can help you land your dream job

WHEN YOU DO WHAT SUCCESSFUL PEOPLE DO, YOU GET WHAT SUCCESSFUL PEOPLE GET

Get your college career off to a flying start by knowing and using basic strategies of successful college students.

MINIMUM SPEED LIMIT

Minimum Speed Limit 45

Show up to class. It's basic. It's expected. Your absence will be noticed. You're investing quite a chunk of change and tons of time to earn a college education.

Go to class every time. Students who start skipping quickly start thinking that class isn't all that important, maybe because unlike high school, no one calls to find out why you've missed. Missing class may feel like freedom, but it is academic suicide.

Pay attention. Take notes. It's the least you can do to get a decent grade.

6 Great Reasons to Go to Class

1. It's expensive to pay and not go.
2. Your professor may put a high premium on attendance.
3. It's a responsible habit that can have long-term payoffs.
4. You will learn more than if you stay away.
5. You get to know other students in the class.
6. It's where the answers are.
   (How else will you know what's on the test?)

THE BAD HABIT THAT CAN LOWER ANY GRADE

In a perfect world, people love learning and continue to read and strive for personal growth throughout their lives. No attention whatsoever is given to grades. What do grades matter in a perfect world, anyway? The joy of learning would be enough to motivate everyone to strive and reach, constantly seeking to be the best they could be.

And yet, this isn't quite a perfect world, and grades DO count, don't they?

You probably do care if you get the "A" over the "B," or the

"B–" over the "C+." For some with dreams of going to graduate school, or for those with scholarships, a lot rides on those magic letters at the end of the term.

Grades are important to you, so they're important to me, and I want to give you the inside scoop on the professor's role in raising your grade.

Throughout this book are tips on earning the best possible grade.

For now, I want to focus on that fraction that often goes unnoticed. Some schools call it the "discretionary" part of the great grade equation. In other words, if the professor thinks a student is apathetic, he might factor in an "F" to that discretionary portion and severely impact the student's grade.

Some say the discretionary fraction accounts for only 10% of your grade. But think of this: if the class has any subjective portion at all, such as presentations, papers, or essay questions on tests, where will the professor's mind be when he's grading something turned in by a student who's absent 80% of the time? And how do you think all of those missed classes will impact that professor as he decides if your essay is a "C" or a "D?"

So, what's the bad habit that can lower any grade? You guessed it. It's skipping class.

Studies show that missing as few as 10% of classes can start to lower a grade. Julia Richardson, a freshman at University of Chicago, told me that her Biology professor got so fed up with people missing the class that he would deliberately tell the students who were there "throwaway" questions that would be on the test. For example, he would say, "See that graph on page 154? I'll ask you a question about that on the test." Finally, people started catching on when they got to the mid-term and were clueless about 20% of the questions.

Get on your professor's good side and stay there.

About 85% of your success in life rests on your ability to get along well with others. This includes gaining and keeping good rapport with the professor. If he likes your attitude, you're much more likely to max out that discretionary 10% that has a significant influence on your grade.

Go early; stay late.

Okay, you don't have to keep sitting there minutes after the class ends. You should, however, come a few minutes early and stay though the entire class. No need to be the last person to leave, just don't create a draft trying to get out the door at the end of class.

How early do you need to come to class? Early enough that you have your book and notepaper out and your pen poised and ready to go before the professor even opens his mouth.

Why?

Because often, he has either just taught a class or just reviewed his notes, and wants to make sure he makes some critical points before they slip his mind. Sometimes, students will be talking to him just before class starts, and maybe they're all asking the same question. He will use those first few moments of class to clear up the issue for the entire class.

Also, your professor may wrap up the class making sure he touches on and reviews key concepts one more time before you go. Remember that key concepts are testable material.

FALLING ROCKS

A tiny transgression that's more damaging than you'd think: coming a little late to class or leaving a little early.

Be aware of the image you project in the classroom. Whether you realize it or not, something as small as coming in a minute late from time to time, or packing up while the professor is still talking and slipping out a moment early makes you look bad.

It suggests disrespect for the professor and the class. Whatever your reason for being late, correct the situation so you can be where you need to be when you need to be there. If you absolutely must be late or leave early because of an appointment, let the professor know ahead of time.

Coming a bit late or leaving a bit early, unless it's absolutely necessary, and you've mentioned it to the professor beforehand, makes you look bad. It may appear that you don't plan your time well, so you can't get there on time. You may seem (gasp!) lazy and thoughtless.

4

Now that may be a lot to read into being late and leaving early, however, all the professor has to go on is what he sees, not your reasons for doing it.

And when you do go to class, BE there. Sit as close to the front as is comfortable, focus, come prepared, and take part in active listening and note taking. When the time is right, jump on in and ask a question. Answer a few, too. It's your class. Make the most of it.

EXPRESSWAY

Expressway 4.0 Stand out in the crowd. Let your professors know you care. Say you're one of 357 students in an intro History class. How do you let your professor know who you are? In three easy steps:

Sit no farther back than the third row, right in the center.

Always look attentive.

Make an appointment early in the semester so you can meet one-on-one with the professor. Ask for some clarification on one of the topics he's been presenting, or for some help narrowing down your focus on a paper you'll write for that class.

Let him know that you are paying attention and care about learning. Introduce yourself soon in the semester. His being able to attach a face to every paper will positively affect every subjective grade he gives you.

WHAT YOUR PROFESSORS WILL NEVER TELL YOU ABOUT CLASS PARTICIPATION

There are such things as stupid questions. And professors inwardly roll their eyes when they hear one.

You've seen this happen. You're in class, and a student who usually sleeps (and snores!) through most of the period, raises a hand and begins, "This is probably a stupid question..." For some reason, the professor answers, "Now, there are no stupid questions." And sure enough, here it comes—the most ridiculous question you've heard all year.

If you're thinking there are such things as stupid questions, you're right. However, to soften the blow, let's call them ill-advised questions.

Let's review questions you don't want to be caught dead asking.

Anytime you do not read the assignment for the day, you may not ask questions.

Why not ask if you haven't read? Quite simply, you can end up really looking silly if the question is already answered in the text. It's a bad mark against you. It makes you look not only ill prepared, but lazy. Your professor is thinking you didn't do your part, and now you want to use class time for something you should have done yourself.

Bad idea.

Also, if you have one of those professors who likes to rub it in

OASIS

The surprising truth about asking for extra credit is that your professors don't think highly of your asking.

Although you are offering to do extra work, it also means the professor must do extra grading. The problem goes beyond that, however. It's just not good form to ask the professor if you can do something extra when you haven't done the basics well. It sends the wrong message.

Bottom line: Don't even bother asking if you can do extra credit.

when it's obvious that a student hasn't prepared, you may be in for some serious teasing throughout the term.

You can also forget getting others to be your partner on a group project. Once others know you don't do your work, they won't want to let you ride on their coattails. And obviously, nobody wants to work in a study group with people who won't carry their own weight, either.

See? Some questions are best left unasked.

Now that I've got some of you sufficiently paranoid, two important points:

- If you have prepared, yes, please do ask a question, if you need a point clarified. Jump right in there.
- If you do ask a question DO NOT, under any circumstance, begin by saying, "This is probably a stupid question..." Be bold. It earns you more respect.

THE DOCTOR IS IN, BUT DON'T PUSH IT

When I was in graduate school at Northeastern University, I took a film class. It was an elective for my Master's in English Literature.

Great class. Watch movies; write papers; get credit. What a treat!

Most films were available in the library, and those that weren't were available in the local video store.

For some reason, this nice film professor offered to let anyone who "couldn't find the film" watch it on his TV in his office. One of my classmates would always go to his office to watch it. I asked if she'd like to borrow my rental. No, she answered, she liked to go to the professor's office because she had a huge crush on him!

Yikes!

I tried suggesting to her that pursuing a happily married professor was, perhaps, a supreme waste of time, but she persisted. He finally ended up telling her he needed to kick her out so he could make phone calls. He eventually stopped letting people use his office to watch the films. I couldn't help but wonder how much the student with the misplaced crush had to do with that decision.

The other point about using office hours is not to use them as a replacement for preparing for class. If you aren't going to prepare for class, sit where you know you can follow the lecture, and actively listen, don't use the professor's entire office time to play catch up. Go with a few key questions, thank the professor, and leave.

Your best bet is to plan visits in advance. Professors usually have little free time. Some only grant office time by appointment, and some allow visits on a first come, first served basis. So, if you do need some help, ask for a specific time, be prompt, come prepared with specific questions, and graciously leave when you're finished.

HOW YOUR PROFESSORS CAN HELP YOU LAND YOUR DREAM JOB

Even if you're the underdog, your grades aren't strait "A's," you aren't the president of student council or the captain of the soccer team, there are terrific professors out there who genuinely enjoy helping sincere, hardworking students who are willing to help themselves.

Professors can boost your academic and professional career.

They can be another source for important inside information for shaping your college career. Meg O'Brien, a psychology major and a sophomore at UCLA, was the top student in her speech class. Her professor told her he would recommend her for a coveted position as a

Teacher's Assistant (TA) for their Master's program. If accepted, she could receive tuition-free education to attend graduate school in the Communications department for teaching only two classes a semester.

She told her professor that, while she appreciated the vote of confidence, she wasn't even pursuing her Bachelor's in Communications. Although she didn't stay for a Master's program, she did switch to Communications for her Bachelor's major, received superb mentoring from a top professor in that field, and went on to begin an exciting assignment in journalism immediately after graduation.

Not only can professors let you in on the top deals offered by the school before the positions are announced publicly, they can also write knock-your-socks-off letters of recommendation to future potential employers, and to graduate schools you may be interested in attending down the road.

You might be surprised at how much influence some of your professors have. Many are very well respected in the community and have long standing ties to local organizations and associations that might prove helpful in your future job or internship search. Some well-established professors also enjoy a positive reputation nation-wide.

I've worked with many students whose professors have mentored them and helped them make the right connections for scholarships, the top graduate schools, and the best job offers. So get on their good side, and stay there.

One way to earn the respect and attention of your professors is to be attentive and make good grades. Let's look at some ways you can balance all of your responsibilities as a college student and do well in all of them.

SHAVE HOURS OFF FUTURE STUDY TIME

Prime your mind to store and retain information. Here are five reasons prepping for class makes learning a whole lot easier.

Big Picture Overview primes memory.

Our memory works by associating new ideas with old ones. When you read the assignment, and review the notes from last class, you pave the way for new information to be connected with this big picture concept that you've just studied.

It gives the mind an overall picture of what the main themes of the class will be. Our brains naturally store and recall information more effectively when we start with a big picture concept of the key ideas, and then fill in with specific examples and applications.

You'll recognize and understand key terms faster.

Remember, understanding key terms and key concepts is the basis for taking brief, memorable notes. For example, say your Psychology class is studying Freud. You need to know about the ego, superego, and the id, and when Freud says they develop. Reviewing ahead of time, you've primed your mind to perk up when your professor mentions any of these key terms. You will be able to listen more carefully, and to take clearer, more memorable notes.

It allows note-taking shorthand.

Reading before class lets you check off directly in your book when the professor covers material in the text. Those unprepared will be writing like mad; you'll simply be putting a symbol beside anything the professor mentions that's in the book. I recommend the letter "c" with a circle around it, so you can quickly notice that this is information covered in class. Anything mentioned both in the book and in the classroom is worth making a special note of.

It primes active listening.

Finally, coming prepared sets you up for active listening. The golden nuggets that you want in your notes are contained within the key words and key concepts in 10% of the lecture.

Let me cover the idea of key words and concepts in more depth here.

Say you just saw a great movie and you want to tell some friends about it. How much do you tell them? Certainly not all the dialogue. In fact, you probably wouldn't mention the dialogue at all unless it contained a funny joke.

Nope, you'd stick with the synopsis—just the highlights. You would condense a two-hour show into a five-minute description.

The review you would give the movie contains the essence of the key words. That's exactly what you'll want to write down when you're taking notes on a lecture—the main ideas, not every word. Imagine that you're going to tell a fellow classmate who had to miss class what the lecture was about. Those ideas you'd share are what you want in your notes.

Prep makes taking notes a lot easier.

Perhaps the best way to take notes is a process of non-linear, one-page note taking, sometimes called brain webs or Mind Maps®. In this process, the central idea is placed in the middle, and the main themes radiate outward with subcategories attached to their respective themes.

When you've looked at the material before class, you have a much better idea of how the key points interconnect. This helps you to write your notes in a way that shows you how the concepts relate to each other.

For more information on *Mind Mapping®*, see Tony Buzan's book on the subject. You'll learn a lot and end up saving yourself tons of time.

CHAPTER 2

PET PEEVES THAT DRIVE PROFESSORS UP THE WALL

DISCOVER:

- **Three questions never to ask your professor**

- **Eight biggest mistakes students make**

- **What not to admit, even when you're being honest**

- **How to avoid zoning out in class**

WHAT YOUR PROFESSORS WANT FROM YOU

In spite of any horror stories you may have heard from friends in school, college professors are only human. They want what you want: respect, attention, appreciation. No great surprises here, right?

Well, what you may not know is that these professors expect you to follow a few unwritten rules about how to be a good college student. I want you to know about these expectations now, before you go and make embarrassing blunders. So read and heed, and avoid making a bad impression and alienating a person who could be a huge help to your academic and professional careers.

Peruse these warnings, commit them to memory, and violate them at your own peril.

STOP

STOP Think twice before you ask the following three questions. Although your intent may be positively innocent, your frustrated professor could hear an entirely different meaning behind your message.

"When is it due?"

"Is this testable?"

"I was gone last class. Did I miss anything important?"

Read on to learn why these are killer questions to avoid at all costs.

THREE QUESTIONS NEVER TO ASK YOUR PROFESSOR

Unless you want to sound like a first semester freshman (all due respect, first semester freshmen), or to set off your professor on a lecture no one wants to hear, make sure you don't ask the following innocent, but ill-advised questions:

"When is it due?" It's in your syllabus, which you, of course, have reviewed diligently so you can plan the next several months around your academic advancement. Asking your professor this question is like asking where your notebook is. It's your job to know.

"Is this testable?" Double whammy if you ask when the professor is on a roll, digressing on some protracted story that lost you 10 minutes ago. Although it seems like an intelligent question at first,

12   © Crystal Jonas

it drives professors crazy. Why? Professors generally have spent copious amounts of time researching to bring you the latest and greatest information about what they teach. Most want to pass on to you their enthusiasm for the subject so you want to learn for the sake of learning itself.

In the real world, you and I know everyone can't love every single class. In some courses you just want to know the bottom line, "Hey, will you ask me this on a test?" Fair enough, from the perspective on your side of the desk. Here's what the professor hears when you ask that question: "Do I need to listen now, or can I zone out again, since I'm bored beyond belief, and I'm only taking this class because there was no way out of it?"

While it may be the case that you are barely able to remain conscious as you listen to the professor pontificate about the topic at hand, remember, diplomacy is paramount when dealing with your professors. And, it's your job to figure out what might be tested by paying close enough attention so you can tell when points are being repeated and emphasized. Your professor isn't generally going to be so blunt as to say, "...and this is on the test." If she does, consider it a gift.

"I was gone last class. Did I miss anything important?" This is actually a common question that, on the surface, seems harmless enough. Aren't you even quite responsible to follow up and ask to make sure you aren't missing out on some crucial point in your education because you didn't attend the last class? Alas, dear student, in spite of your best intentions about making up for lost time in following up on any goodies missed, here's what the professor hears, "Did you say anything I'll be tested on?" or worse, "You don't usually say anything important, was last Tuesday an exception?" Sadly, either way, you don't end up looking very good. And oh, by the way, you already missed class, so what's up with that?

I know...it cuts to the core to be misunderstood. What's a well-meaning, conscientious student supposed to do when he misses a class? Ask for the notes of a couple of friends, and review them. As long as you have also read the material necessary for the class you missed, make an appointment to see the professor so you can make sure you have a clear understanding of what you see as the main concepts.

Since you're showing initiative, and will have great questions to ask, your professor will be much more receptive to helping you and filling in those missing pieces. Don't expect a complete rehashing of the class, but with your prep, this session could be enough to make up for the missed class.

By the way, there are only a few legitimate reasons for missing class. If you go in for extra help after missing a class, make sure it falls within the "true emergency" category. If your reason doesn't pass muster, (and sorry, an *American Idol* marathon doesn't count) don't even try to make an appointment with the professor for extra help. You'll just call attention to your absence even more.

SLOW DOWN

> SLOW
>
> While we're on the topic of questions that shouldn't be asked, think twice before asking: "Can we leave early today?"
>
> It's so tempting to ask when spring fever hits, or you've got tickets to a concert and a 2 hour drive to get there. Seems like a harmless enough request, right?
>
> You know the problem? It rubs most professors the wrong way. Completely without malice, you offer a great idea, "Hey, let's get out of here early today so we can all enjoy the sunshine."
>
> Here's what your professor hears: "I'd really rather be anywhere else than here. So, rather than take the initiative to skip class, I want you to give me permission to leave, and while you're at it, give everyone else the "all clear" to leave with me so I don't miss anything."

I remember the Dark Ages, when I was an undergrad, I had a course with a classmate who always seemed to arrive late, leave early, and ask to be cut loose before the end of class. One day, I found out when I got to class that John Lennon had been fatally shot (Yes, I'm that old.). The professor, a huge Beatles fan, came in five minutes late (he'd never been late before), wearing dark glasses. Somberly, he opened his notebook, and read the words to Lennon's moving song, "Imagine." Less than three seconds after he finished reciting, this classmate asked, "So, does this mean we get out of class early today?" The professor just shook his head, closed his notebook, and walked out.

Not only did she burn her reputation with a really great professor, but she also lost the respect of her classmates.

BIGGEST MISTAKES STUDENTS MAKE

- Asking the "forbidden questions" mentioned above (They make you look like a beginner—or someone who should know better, but doesn't.)
- Not reading the syllabus (Professors put a lot of time and thought into these, you can at least read them and know what's expected of you.)
- Making excuses instead of taking responsibility (Very high school, and you left that behind long ago.)
- Trying to get by on charm instead of merit (Don't try to be the teacher's pet. Not only does it annoy professors, it annoys your fellow classmates, too.)
- Turning in assignments late (This sends all the wrong messages. You have as much time as anyone else. Get it done and hand it in on time. No excuses.)
- Asking to make up a test (Think about this one. The professor has to make a whole new test in this case. Not at all a fun thing to do. And how happy do you think she's going to be when she writes and grades it? Make it to the regularly scheduled test time whatever the cost.)
- Asking for help when it's far too late (Make an appointment at your first clue that you may need some extra guidance.)
- Popping in for office hours without an appointment (Many professors prefer to schedule people so they know what to expect and can plan their time better. No "pop-ins" please. Getting on their calendar and being on time shows that you're serious about doing well, and it shows respect for their time.)

WHAT NEVER TO ADMIT TO A PROFESSOR

Never, ever admit that you hate the class. I do not care if you consider the admission, as one misinformed student said, "just being honest." While just being honest is normally a noble trait, there's no need to have full disclosure about something that might offend the person with the power to flunk you, or to make the semester very unpleasant.

Think for a moment about how many brain cells your professor has sacrificed on the academic alter to get her PhD (or Master's, for that matter) in her chosen field.

For years, she gave up watching television, spending time with friends, and reading books with no social redeeming value so that she could devote her time to study, write and research, days, months, and years on end to immerse herself in this particular subject.

Now, you're going to moan and groan about how this course has nothing to do with your chosen career field, and you can't for the life of you understand why anyone in her right mind would make her life's work in this silly subject for Pete's sake, and why, oh why, couldn't you just take only those classes that really appeal to your inner Einstein?

Let me give you some tough love here. A college education purposefully exposes you to a well-rounded education.

A balanced curriculum is one of the great benefits of advanced education. To complain about a class and go on about how you don't see its value not only insults the person who has made it the nucleus of her work, it also makes it look like you don't "get" the concept of higher education. Such is not a great way to impress your professor.

So drop the editorial, suck it up, and get on with the class! It's only a semester out of your life; you'll knock it out and be done with it in no time.

YIELD

YIELD — Raise your awareness about how your professor feels about her chosen career field. Too many clueless students have innocently stated that they can't stand the class they're in, nor can they fathom why they have to be subjected to the torture of taking the class when they can see not even a glimmer of value in it.

What in the world would possess them to say such a thing right in front of the professor? Not only in her presence, but also sometimes, right to her face? Who knows? Just don't you be one of those clueless college students who runs like a bulldozer over the professor by going on about how stupid and useless the class is. It will only reflect poorly on you.

Your professor's impression of you, like it or not, will be consciously or subconsciously in her mind every single time she grades one of your assignments or tests. Also, as we learned earlier, professors can help us make contacts in the real world of great internships and dream careers. Give your instructor every opportunity to think the best of you.

Okay, even if you do not totally love the class, you still need to go and look conscious—if not riveted and hanging on every word uttered from the brilliant mind that is your professor. Not always an easy task, I'll be the first to admit.

Few things are more obvious and insulting to a professor than a student who gets the glazed over, zoned out look that screams: "I'm about to crash and burn from lack of sleep and interest." If you're about to fall asleep, you're kidding no one, least of all, your professor. Still, your looking alive is part of what the professor expects, so make sure you're getting plenty of rest so you can be alert and ready to learn during class time.

HOW TO KEEP FROM ZONING OUT IN CLASS

Let's face it: not all classes will keep you glued to the edge of your seat with unflinching interest. Sometimes either the subject matter isn't your favorite, or you stayed up late last night, or perhaps both.

How in the world are you going to make it through class without doing the head bob ten minutes into it?

First, if you aren't opposed to consuming large quantities of caffeine, go for it. Bring a monster ultra big slurp of soda or a shot of espresso to class. Caffeine has helped a great many college students through those challenging times of burning the midnight oil or suffering through interminable classes with mind-numbing subject matter and humorless professors.

Drink up. If you can sneak some snacks without the professor giving you the evil eye, do so. I suggest something with a shock of flavor, like those super sour chewy worms. They will keep your taste buds awake and, one hopes, you with them.

Now that you're awake, and you've chosen to go to class rather than skip (kudos to you, by the way) make sure you're sitting up close (no farther back than the third row, or you may find yourself too easily distracted) and take notes with colored pencils or markers to keep your mind visually stimulated and increase the likelihood that you'll remember what you write down.

DETOUR

DETOUR ➡ What's that you say? You got behind the eight ball and didn't (in spite of my gentle warnings) read your assignment before going to class, and now you're thinking that it's best to just skip class and catch up on your reading during class time?

No, no, dear reader. Skipping class because you aren't prepared is the common pitfall of the novice, and since you have the great foresight to read this book you know that the last thing you want to do is to compound the mistake of not prepping for class with the misguided choice of also missing the class.

So, go to class, be on time, sit close, listen actively, take notes, and catch up on your reading—post haste!

While in class actively listen, and begin asking yourself questions as you take thoughtful, well-chosen notes on the main ideas the professor imparts. Here are some questions you may want to ask as you jot down some ideas on paper:

- What are the key words, phrases, and concepts in today's lecture?
- How does this fit in with the section of homework I read before coming to class?
- How does this new information connect with what I already know about this topic?
- If I were making a test that covered today's lesson, which questions would I ask?
- Given the questions I'd put on the test, what would the answers be?
- What themes and key ideas does the professor emphasize?

Look for ideas that are repeated. Notice any shift in language, such as your professor's voice suddenly becoming louder or softer, in order to get the class's attention, or a verbal clue such as, "most importantly," or "the bottom line is that..." Note too, a dramatic shift in body language, such as turning around from writing on the board, taking off the glasses, pausing for effect. Learn how to read your professor; she'll tell you nonverbally, if not straight out, if something is especially important.

Keep asking yourself questions and challenging yourself to find smart answers. Keep your mind actively engaged in the material. And if it's okay by your professor, and it usually is, keep sipping that extra large-quad-shot latte. The caffeine should keep you alert.

CHAPTER 3

HOW TO GET BETTER GRADES WITH LESS EFFORT

DISCOVER:

- **Four-factor formula for learning anything faster**

- **Golden rules of rapid reading**

- **The most common mistake of speed readers**

- **Where to find clues to what's on your next test**

- **Three reading speed bumps you must overcome**

- **Reading myths that muddle memory**

- **TREATS that make you a better reader**

FOUR-FACTOR FORMULA FOR LEARNING ANYTHING FASTER

Before you jump right in to all that reading, and as you've learned by now, you will have a ton of reading to do in college, before you sit down to a huge pile of books and notes to study, prepare yourself to read and recall this material as quickly and easily as possible.

There are four factors in the formula that prepares you for accelerated learning:

Be sure you are:

1. Comfortable
2. Confident
3. Clear
4. Curious

First, make sure you can read in a comfortable place. The more technical the information is, the more important this point is. You can read a great fiction novel standing in a blizzard at a bus stop and never notice the weather. I can't say that you'd be equally tuned out to your surroundings if the book in your hand weren't the latest best-seller, but that mega-sized world history text.

Ideally, sit in a padded upright chair. Yes, it does have to be an upright chair. You and I both know what's going to happen in you prop yourself up on your bed to tackle this task. You'll stretch out with your highlighters, textbook, and the best intentions, and before you know it, your alarm clock is waking you up for your first morning class.

Know the difference between getting comfortable and getting casual.

If you stretch out on your bed, propped up against several pillows, your mind thinks you're not very serious about this whole study thing. The whole lie-down-on-the-bed-and-go-to-sleep pattern is pretty deeply ingrained. Make sure you are sitting up and ready to read. Choose a chair with a straight back and your brain will get that you are getting down to business. Try it yourself. You may be surprised at the difference it makes in helping you stay alert and focused.

Second, be confident in your ability to learn anything and everything you need to know to be successful. This book may be the first time you've been exposed to the information about how powerful your mind is. You truly do have the mind of a genius. You've got more than a trillion brain cells. All you need to do is find out how to use all of that mind power, and then put it to use to make learning easier and a lot more fun.

Third, when you're preparing to learn quickly, be clear about what you want to understand and recall. Think about what the syllabus says the class is going to be about. Create some questions that will help you make the most of the time you spend reading and reviewing the material. The more specific you are about what you want to learn, the easier it will be to focus in on exactly what you want, and skim over what you don't need to know.

Finally, be curious. Curiosity implies that you actually want to learn about the topic. It puts you in the driver's seat for studying, and lets you know that you are actually spending all this time on this topic because you're interested. Curiosity also keeps you open-minded to learn new concepts. Curiosity allows you to ask many specific questions. These will focus your attention and prepare you to quickly recognize the answer when you come across it.

THE SECRET BEHIND SPEED READING

RUSH HOUR

Got a ton of reading to do and wondering how you're going to get it all done? Take a deep breath and follow these simple steps.

Be confident in your brain's ability to cover and comprehend the reading.

Know before you start how much you'll cover, and what you want to get out of the material.

Preview all headings first.

Read any questions at the end of the chapter.

Ask yourself as you read: "What are the main ideas here? How do they fit in with what I already know about this topic?"

Jot your own form of notes and symbols in the margins.

Stop every 20 minutes or so to quiz yourself on what you've just read.

Unless what you're reading is completely technical and foreign to you, slowing down to read takes away from understanding the material.

I know. You've been taught that slowing down will help you understand the material better. Alas, not so.

Your brain passes over those words and understands their meaning much faster than your eyes can see them and that little voice in your head can say them in your mind.

Reading faster allows you to take in all this material in a way that is more meaningful for your brain.

When it comes to speed reading, here's the secret: Rapid reading has nothing to do with how many words you take in. It's all about how many ideas you can process and retain. People new to speed reading get so wrapped up in how many pages they're covering, they have a hard time retaining the main ideas. They haven't primed their minds to grasp and remember the key concepts in what they're reading.

To prevent falling into the beginning speed- reader trap, focus on these GOLDEN RULES OF RAPID READING

- Read in chunks. By that, I mean focus on about 3 words at a time. Let your brain process them as a unit.
- Read for ideas; forget caring about the number of words you're covering.

FALLING ROCKS

The most common mistake of speed readers: Some people who are really into the whole speed reading thing start bragging about how many words per minute they can read. Guess what folks? That's not the point.

The goal of academic reading at any speed is to comprehend key concepts, and recall it when you need it. Period.

Instead of caring how many words per minute you're reading, concentrate on how many ideas you're taking in.

WHERE TO FIND CLUES TO WHAT'S ON YOUR NEXT TEST

Your goals of reading are to understand, recall, synthesize, and apply.

Obviously, all of this reading isn't going to do you any good if you have absolutely no clue what all of those words mean. Slow it down; take in all the clues, including any charts, graphs, and pictures. Any good textbook will offer tons of visual cues to let you know what information is most important. (And yes, most of the books you will buy for school will be quite good.)

The authors want to make sure they give the most important ideas plenty of "ink" and the more complex concepts plenty of explanation. So, you will find the really important stuff noted in headlines, addressed several times, and possibly, further explained in drawings, charts, and tables.

Anything that the authors of your books spend extra time explaining in the formats mentioned here is a clear indication of what's really important in the text. If your professor relies on the textbook at all (and many do) these clues in the text tell you key concepts that are fair game for your next test.

So, if there ever is anything that your textbook is emphasizing by putting the information in headlines, drawings, charts, or tables, and you're not quite understanding it, be sure to ask the professor to help you understand the material. Chances are very good you'll see it again on a test.

YIELD

As tempting as it may be to jump right in to those 150 pages of homework you're expected to read tonight, slow down and invest less than six minutes to save yourself tons of time in the long run.

A big part of memory works by linking new information with information you already have locked in your mind. Spend just a few moments reviewing all of the information you can recall about the topic you're about to study.

You can think about what you've recently been hearing in class, as well as what you've learned reading about the topic on your own. This tiny bit of time invested allows you to take in this new information more quickly and to be better able to retrieve the information later at some important moment, for example, at test time!

It's important that you review what you already know about the topic you're about to study before focusing on new information. In doing this, you come away with a deeper understanding and memory of the material because you've synthesized, or merged, the new information with the material about that topic that you already have stored in long-term memory. And there you sit, smarter, and with less effort.

THREE READING SPEED BUMPS YOU *MUST* OVERCOME

Speed Bump # 1: Sub-vocalizing

If you're like most college students I've talked with, you sub-vocalize and don't even notice it. Not many people realize that A) this is quite common, B) most people don't even know that they are doing it, and C) it is a major factor in slowing down the reading process.

Sub-vocalizing isn't the same as reading the words aloud to yourself; it's not even moving your lips, although if you do either of these, of course, you're slowing yourself down even more. It refers to hearing each word mentally, sounding them out in your head. It's really a holdover from when we first learned to read and we hold on to this habit mainly because we've never been taught that our brains can comprehend without hearing the words in our heads. Interesting, isn't it?

Some poetry lovers out there are going to say that some writings were meant to be read slowly, savoring the sound of each word either in the head or aloud. They are right. Some writings are created specifically to have the sounds they make enjoyed slowly and deliberately.

This doesn't not, however, apply to most of what you'll be expected to read and recall in college.

For most of the material you will cover, it doesn't matter how it sounds, only what the meaning is behind the words. You make the judgment call. If you're reading poetry, sub-vocalize away. Hey, you might even enjoy reading aloud. Just make sure you stop saying each word in your head after you put away the poetry.

Solution to Speed Bump #1: Move your finger over the words faster than you can say them in your head. Make your mind follow along. Although it will feel funny at first, you'll quickly see that you can process meaning that quickly, without even saying each word in your head.

Speed Bump #2: Backtracking

Funny thing is, in our culture, we have almost a reverence for the written word. Think about how hard it is to throw away a book.

If we think we've missed a word on that last line, most of us will go back and reread that entire line.

And yet, that is completely unnecessary.

Why? Well, if it's a really important point, you will get more than one chance to read it. Think about it. The important stuff is in the headlines, or subheads, illustrated in a chart, graph, or picture of some sort. It may be included in a list, appear as a caption to an illustration, or be further explained in several examples.

Face it. The important information is always repeated. So, sit tight and rest assured that if you missed one word that unlocks the secrets of the universe, you will read that word again. And besides, what are the odds that the secrets of the universe really will be revealed in that one tiny word you just skimmed over?

Solution to Speed Bump #2: Put an index card over the line you've just read to prevent going back over it again.

EXPRESSWAY

Expressway 4.0

Going back and rereading words that you believe you missed is called backtracking. Instead of reading that slowly and carefully, speed up instead. Stopping to backtrack over what you believe are missed ideas will impair your brain's natural ability to process, comprehend, and retain information quickly.

You'll find yourself remembering a lot more if increase your speed and let your mind take in the ideas faster so it can follow how the details fit together without your eyes hindering the process.

Speed Bump #3: Reading without purpose

Read this next idea very closely. I hope that you go into every academic reading assignment with a clear idea of how much you will read, and what you are looking to get out of your investment of time.

You are investing time when you read and, considering the many books you'll labor over in school, you'll want to have a clear idea about exactly what you want to get out of each and every reading assignment. Approach each assignment with a clear goal.

Know how much you're going to read and ask yourself some questions to help direct your focus. If you haven't covered these basic necessities, you're not ready to read. Put the book down, and go do something else. There's really no reason to waste your time until you are ready to get down to reading with a purpose.

Solution to Speed Bump #3: Remember that a major secret in studying smarter in a shorter amount of time is to begin with a clear purpose because when you know what you're looking for, you're more likely to find it. Makes sense, doesn't it?

As you're reading, you can speed up the process and your ability to quickly comprehend what's being said by keeping a lookout on words that are major clues in what's important in the text.

"More of the same" clues: "also," "likewise," "furthermore," "additionally," "moreover." These words signal that nothing new follows. If you already get the point and how it applies, press on.

"Change in direction, contradiction" clues: "however," "although," "but," "on the other hand," "rather," "nevertheless." Perk up. This signals a new perspective on what you've just read.

"In a nutshell" clues: "in sum," "in short," "therefore," "in conclusion." Slow down, take it all in. This sums it all up. Always read what follows. It's a great opportunity to review.

READING MYTHS THAT MUDDLE MEMORY

The myth: Slow down.

The truth: This will interfere with your fast-working brain's ability to process information. (The exception: If the material is especially technical or unfamiliar to you, read more slowly.)

The myth: Don't use your finger to direct your eyes along the page.

The truth: It can keep you from sub-vocalizing the words. The technique: Move your finger or a pen along the page at a brisk rate so you don't give yourself a chance to say the words, yet your mind continues to quickly process the concepts.

(The exception: You may want to keep doing this no matter how fast you get. Most seasoned speed readers still use their hands to direct their eyes over the page.)

The myth: Look up words as you go.

The truth: This will slow you down and discourage you. The solution: Mark the word, and look for the meaning in the context. Remember, all of the important ideas are repeated and further illustrated and explained.

Sample questions to help focus your attention while you read:

What is the main idea?

What are the key concepts?

How does this relate to what else I know about the topic?

What opinions, if any, did the author present?

TREATS WILL HELP YOU BE A BETTER READER

Each letter in the word TREATS will help you prepare your mind to read with greater focus, comprehension, and sustained concentration than ever.

The letters in the acronym TREATS stand for:

- Topic
- Related points
- Element of Uniqueness
- Angle
- Thoughts
- So what?

Let's take these one at a time.

Before you even pick up that book, think about the **topic**. What do you already know about it? Given the reading assignment, what do you think the general theme will be?

Once you have an appreciation of the main idea, begin to think of **related points**. Recall that we remember by associating new thoughts with what we already know. By thinking about what you already know about this topic, you provide a framework to which you can attach this new information.

Next, move on to consider the **elements of uniqueness** in your reading. This tunes your mind to read much more actively and to stay involved in the material. You don't need to read the material very closely at all if it covers stuff you already know. Be looking for a fresh example, a new perspective, and get something valuable out of the reading experience.

When you look for the *angle*, you consider the slant or bias of the book's author. Also, ask yourself: "What would my professor find important about this topic? How does this fit in with what the class has been discussing?" Finding the angle makes you a much sharper reader.

Before you read, generate your own *thoughts* on the topic. Articulate clear questions on what you want to get out of the assignment. Keep in mind that the more clear you are, the more likely you are to get what you want out of the session.

Ask, *so what?* How does this fit in with the big picture of what the semester is going to be about? Continue to ask the "so what?" question every time you read. You will train your mind to be thinking: "What am I supposed to get from this?" In doing so, you'll comprehend and retain much more information.

As you zip through the TREATS exercise, you prepare yourself to read much more quickly and with greater comprehension than you would otherwise have. The five minutes you spend on this little exercise will greatly justify your minimal mental investment.

CHAPTER 4

DISCOVER THE SIMPLE SECRETS OF SMART STUDENTS

DISCOVER:

- Key times when most test answers are given away

- Twelve ways to pass a killer class

- The document that guides you to an "A"

- A caveat before contact

- Quickly write a paper the professor will love

- The 10% of the lecture that's noteworthy

KEY TIMES WHEN MOST TEST ANSWERS ARE GIVEN AWAY

While it's true that doing well in school is a whole lot easier than you imagined, it still does take some attention on your part.

The key to getting good grades without killing yourself studying until the wee hours of the morning is to make sure you're doing the right thing at the right time.

Make the most of every minute.

Want better test scores? Of course you do.

Here's a tip for boosting your grade that has nothing to do with cracking the books. While this is not to say you can avoid studying all together, you can give your scores a boost, many times a huge boost if you know a few tricks.

One of the biggest bonuses in this bag of tricks is to reap the benefits of going to class. Remember that when it comes to going to class, you'll want to:

- Go
- Go every time
- Stay the whole time

The first few and the last few moments of class happen to be when professors reveal key ideas that you just might see on those exams you'll be taking.

For some reason, many students think it's not a big deal to be "fashionably late" to class. If you ever slip into that mindset, have a friend bop you upside the head with a rolled-up newspaper. It's very poor form to be late. It sends a rude message to your professor that suggests you're just far too busy, or scattered, to make it to class on time.

Smart students know that a lot of terrific testable tips roll off the top of the professor's head into the opening points of the class lecture. If you waltz in late, don't expect that it will be repeated, or that your fellow classmates will want to cover for you by telling you what you missed.

Sometimes, professors will end class with several testable nuggets that all the people who skipped out early or skipped out all together will miss. This may happen often with professors who allow a lot of discussion, leaving the last few minutes of class as the ideal time to emphasize the key points that haven't been brought out in the course of the class.

Finally, some professors feel especially bugged when students cut class, so they reward the students who bothered to come to class (and stay the entire time) by giving them some exact information about what will be on the test. The students who come don't bother to tell the students who missed the class, because that will ruin their chance to make a better grade and end up on the better side of the grading curve. This actually happens!

Make sure you make a habit of going to class all the time, being on time, and staying the whole time. Your professor will notice and good fortune will smile on you.

DETOUR

DETOUR → Skipping class the first week because someone told you nothing important is covered in that time is a good way to take a time-consuming detour off of your shortcut path to college success. Not only will the professor very likely go over the syllabus with you, but you're absence those first few classes will be forever etched in your professor's memory. Not a good first impression to overcome.

12 WAYS TO PASS A KILLER CLASS

Not all classes are fun-filled, and some are downright unpleasant, especially if one happens to be your worst subject to begin with (and the school's worst professor is the only one teaching it). Before you sign up, explore these ideas.

You have more options than you thought. Here are 12 possibilities that may help you sidestep the class altogether. However, if you can't miss it completely, there are some very practical strategies to make it as painless as possible.

Let's look at each of these in detail:

Avoid it

Completely avoid the class. First ask yourself, "Is there any way out of this class?" Could you take a similar class, perhaps from another department? The curriculum at any school is too extensive for you to know all the details about what class can serve as a suitable substitute

Registration is a busy time on any college campus. Plan ahead and make sure you know all of your options. Before you sign up and suffer through a class you'd really rather not take, try one or more of these suggestions:

- Avoid it
- Plan a "do over"
- Save it for the summer
- Go away
- Prep with a prerequisite course
- Time it right
- Pick the prof you'd prefer
- Get up close and personal
- Preview and review
- Practice pit bull persistence
- Divide and conquer
- Think payoff

for another. Your academic advisor should know if someone in the past has gotten a waiver to take another similar class instead. Perhaps you could, too.

Plan a "do over"

You might not expect it, but auditing a required class you know for a fact will give you trouble will actually save you time in the long run. Your double exposure to the class will allow you to be in a position to master the material when you're taking it for credit. Imagine the time and anguish you will save yourself both times you take the class! The first time because you know you get a "do over" and the second time because it's now all review.

Auditing is definitely an advanced technique for the truly serious students who know exactly what they want and have the awareness to recognize when they are going to need a second pass over the material.

If your GPA is your primary concern because you're headed to graduate school, medical, or law school after graduation, it just might be worth your time and money to audit the class first. So, you'd pay for the class and could attend all lectures, turn in homework, and take the test, but your grade wouldn't count.

Save it for the summer

If you don't want to take the class because it's a particularly difficult one, but it's a non-negotiable requirement, such as Organic Chemistry for pre-med majors, see if it's offered in the summer. The big advantages for this:

The classes will usually be smaller.

You'll get more individualized attention.

You probably won't be taking other classes at the same time.

Not as many people hang around in the summer, and your chances of getting more one-on-one extra assistance time with the professor are much greater.

Go away

Think the course might be a bit of a reach for you? Consider if it's worth your investment to take the course at a local community college. Yes, you're right. This does take time and money. Only you can decide if the payoff is worth it. When do I recommend doing this? Again, when you've got your heart set on graduate school, grades count. A community college may offer the class at a more introductory level than the one you will take at the university.

Do the rewards justify the sacrifice? Only you can decide.

If you're looking for the top internships, grad schools, and job offers, they won't care or even know that you took a prerequisite you didn't need, but that "D" or "F" that you might get if you don't take this step would be hard to explain. It's your choice.

Prep with a prerequisite course

Before diving in head first to a course that could be way over your head, try taking a course that will help you review the basics so the more advanced concepts come a lot easier.

Sometimes, students' academic backgrounds or their tests scores put them in a position to take a more advanced class than they might feel comfortable with. It may be better to take the prerequisite for the more advanced class, after all. Ask your academic advisor or, better yet, the professor who teaches the more advanced class to advise you.

Yes, you're right. It will take extra time to do this review course first. However, imagine the stress it will relieve you of in the long run.

Time it right

If you must take that killer class, make sure you control the time of day that you take it, if you can. Take the class as close to your peak energy time as possible.

Some students completely fade out after lunch. If this is true for you, forget about trying to endure the class between 1:00 and 3:00.

If you can swing it, give yourself extra study time after this class, and don't immediately schedule another class right after it. This will allow the crucial time right after class to take a few minutes to review your notes and let the new information sink in before you have to rush off and learn something else. Also, the extra time will allow you the chance to get some extra assistance with your professor after class if she's available.

Pick the prof you'd prefer

If the class you're dreading is part of the core requirements, chances are very good that several different professors offer it. Check around to find out which professor has the best reputation for teaching this class. There are some really terrific professors out there who can turn a boring, impossible subject into one that's easy to understand and even fun. On the other hand, get the wrong professor, and the class could be a real nightmare.

Get a recommendation from your advisor, too. If your school has a file of past tests grouped by instructor, check out the differences among instructors before you sign up. An enthusiastic, caring professor who uses different ways of getting the material across could make all of the difference in the world.

Get up close and personal

Sit close to the front in class. Face it; students in the back are more easily distracted. I know it sounds so high school, but many will actually whisper and pass notes throughout class. The professor will notice this, and it won't help you get on her good side. Sit closer to the front for the obvious reason. It's kind of hard to process the material if you can't hear it in the first place.

You don't need to sit in the front row, but closeness counts. Studies show that students perform better when they're up front. This is probably because they're more aware when the temptation to zone out comes that they are in full view of the professor who will determine their grades. Also, the professor can interact with students better when they're up front, and can have the chance to read the non-verbal cues that say, "I have absolutely no idea what you just said; please rephrase it."

It's like being in a small group tutorial session.

Preview and review

Always, always prepare for class. Read the material. Review your notes. After class, review your notes again. By reading the material mentioned in the syllabus before class, and rereading your class notes, your brain will be primed for picking up new information and you will be moving all of that information squarely into long-term memory.

Also, doing this kind of preparation before class means that you will be better able to recognize the stuff in the class lecture that's really important. (If it's in the book, and mentioned in the lecture, it's probably important.) This way, you'll know better what to include in your notes. Picking out the key concepts will allow you to write less and remember more. And we are big fans of working less and remembering more.

Finally, about five to ten minutes after class, look through your notes again. A few minutes after we learn anything, our minds are even better prepared for storing the information into long-term memory.

Follow this simple suggestion and you'll find yourself studying less and retaining more.

Practice pit bull persistence

Stay current; stay completely on top of anything you need to read, review, or turn in for this class. Do not even let a single class go by without asking for clarification immediately if there's something you don't quite follow.

Plan from the start to make office visits to the professor on a reasonable schedule. You may not need to go as much as once a week, but go as much as you can to get extra help with the material.

Let your professor know it's your goal to learn as much as you can, and you think you may need a bit of extra help. If you are coming to class prepared, and making an honest effort to stay on top of it, most professors will be happy as clams to offer you some extra insight to help you understand the subject.

Know for now that you always want to be current in classes you suspect you'll be weak in, because getting behind is a sure ticket to a term spent in stress and uncertainty. And who needs that?

Divide and conquer

Get others to study for you! Find out if there's a study group and get in it early. The divide and conquer process will make the class easier to understand and probably more fun, too. Only you can tell if the group is serious enough for you to be worth your time. Not all are, so be sure to be on the lookout for one that serves your purposes.

If you go to a study group, and you know more about the subject than anyone else in the clan, you're in the wrong place. Set your ego aside, and get in with a group that has people who are more comfortable with the topic than you are.

You may find that you want to form your own study group. If this is the case, make sure that you choose carefully. Pick people who know more about the subject than you do, who are serious about doing well, and who will pull their own weight. Think twice about asking your best friend to join the group if he doesn't meet these requirements.

Think payoff

Finally, occasionally give yourself a pep talk about how much your degree means to you and that this class will, eventually, be over.

FALLING ROCKS

Don't be the most knowledgeable person in your study group.

While knowing more than anybody in your group can be a big rush to the ego, it's a real waste of time. The whole point of the study group is to get ideas and insights from others about a topic you're not so sure about.

Two points here:

If you know so much about the topic that you're head and shoulders above everyone else in the group, you can study this subject on your own.

If you really do need help in the class and you're pretty much clueless about the subject, why would you want to be in a group that knows even less about it than you do?

Save your social time for clearly-marked downtime, and get in with a group that has a bunch of eggheads in it so you can learn from others.

Visualize the goal. Follow the other suggestions in this book, and you're sure to make it through even the toughest academic demons.

THE DOCUMENT THAT GUIDES YOU TO AN "A"

If you want to do your best in school, make sure you appreciate the value of the syllabus. Professors pass these out the first day of class to let you know what to expect from them and what they expect from you.

Let's spend a few minutes going over the wealth of information in this little handout so you can fully appreciate its importance to you.

EXPRESSWAY

Expressway 4.0
You may be able to get your professor's syllabus from her website before the term even starts. If you want to get a jump on planning out your semester, look it up, print it out, and read it over.

If it's not posted, ask the professor directly for it. You'll make a great impression before the semester begins and you'll have a head start few, if any, of your classmates have even considered.

Avoid looking irresponsible by making sure you keep your syllabus where you can always find and refer to it. Losing this critical guide and having to ask for another one makes you look like you don't take basic responsibility for your own learning.

Although occasionally, your professor may make a minor change to the syllabus, you can pretty much count on the document laying out what you can expect over the course of the term. Follow it closely and you'll be well on your way to earning your "A."

As soon as you get that syllabus, make sure you read it carefully. Follow this checklist to make sure you're getting all the information you need out of the syllabus:

Highlight:
- Professor's name
- Office location
- Office hours
- Phone number

- E-mail
- Text(s)
- Supplies
- General Information
- Instructions regarding assignments
- Grading criteria (how much assignments, quizzes, and tests will be worth.)
- Attendance policy
- Course schedule

A CAVEAT BEFORE CONTACT

Your professor gave you his contact information because he understands that you may need to reach him outside of class. Here are a few guidelines to help you make thoughtful use of your professor's contact information.

First, make sure you keep and safeguard the information telling you how to reach your professor. Sometimes, it's tempting to think, "I never ask my professors for help. I don't need to track their office hours and location."

Stop.

Think again. You never know when you will find yourself in a real bind and need to contact the professor pronto.

A quick note about the professor's contact information. If he does give out his home number, I don't recommend that you use it, except in extreme emergency. Make sure you conduct your school business during business hours.

Before sending e-mail, be sure to spell check and to give it a quick read before sending it off. Many students have been embarrassed when they later discovered that they sent off a message riddled with spelling errors, or (yikes!) one that they thought they were sending to someone else.

When calling a professor, make sure to plan out what you'll say. That way if you get voice mail, (which very well may happen) you can leave a concise and articulate message.

To plan a voice mail, be sure to leave:
- Your name
- The time and date you called

- Why you're calling
- What you'd like to happen next such as:
  - Call you back (Leave your own number SLOWLY!)
  - Let you know when you might make an office visit
  - Tell you a better time to call when he might be in the office

Few people leave professional sounding voice mail. If you do, you will make a positive impression on the professor, and stand out in a positive way among the dozens of calls she gets each week.

Be sure to get all texts and supplies necessary for the class.

The general information section gives you some insight into the professor's approach for the course. You may also discover in that section what the professor wants you to get from this class, as well.

Read the information regarding assignments carefully. Here, you find out how strict your professor is about getting assignments in on time. You will look and feel silly if this section clearly states that late work isn't accepted and you ask if you can turn your first paper in after it's due.

Some students will read only the "grading criteria" of the syllabus. While this is certainly an important section, it isn't the only one you'll want to read.

What you get from the grading criteria section is a feel for what your final grade will consist of. This may include quizzes, a mid-term, projects, and a final exam. You may even find that class attendance is factored in to the grade. Make sure you know, and even if it isn't specifically listed, you will get much better grades if you go to class.

Make sure that you read the assignments listed before going to class.

After you have gotten your syllabi, make sure you mark all graded assignments, quizzes, and tests on your calendar. Most students I talk with prefer the larger month-at-a-time calendar, since it allows them to mark the information for all of their classes and to see how the next few weeks are shaping up.

It's amazing how much of doing well in school is just a matter of following instructions and being prepared. Do these things and you are already doing more than the average college student.

QUICKLY WRITE A PAPER YOUR PROFESSOR WILL LOVE

- Use a non-linear, "Mind Map"® method of getting some ideas down on paper
- Notice where the strongest clusters lie, and chose your subtopics based on the strongest points to support your thesis statement.
- Say it like you'd say it. Too many students who aren't confident with their writing abilities go way overboard to try to sound highbrow. I call this writing English-ese. It's painful to read and even more painful to write. When you get stuck for words, stop trying so hard. Think out loud, saying exactly what you're trying to write. Then type it just like that. Clarity is paramount.

THE 10% OF A LECTURE THAT IS NOTEWORTHY

Your professor is a lot like you. When she talks, she gets on a roll, gets a little distracted, can digress, and even likes to tell an occasional story or joke that may or may not have anything at all to do with the topic at hand (and that may or may not actually be funny).

Bottom line, don't write down most of what you hear during the course of a lecture. Notice when the professor is going off tangent, and when you can put your pen down for a moment and just listen.

Now, this isn't to say that only 10% is valuable. Not at all. The point is that some students get so caught up in writing down absolutely everything, that they miss the big picture. They capture every word on paper, but they have no idea of the significance of those words.

So what part is noteworthy? Only the 10% that contains the key concepts and ideas needs to make it into your notes.

Imagine that you were going to go to a friend who missed this class and you were going to give the highlights. What would those points be? Of course, not every example, nor every story that helps to illustrate the point. You'd only give the main ideas, and how they interrelate. And there you have it: the small section of the lecture that's noteworthy.

Okay, here's the disclaimer: if you think this means you can blow off the rest of the lecture, you're missing the point. The rest of the class helps you more fully understand those key concepts and put them into perspective with the other material you've learned so far. So, although you don't have to learn a new form of shorthand to get down every word the professor utters, you do want to stay attentive the entire class so you can begin to truly comprehend and store the material for ready recall whenever you need it in the future.

CHAPTER 5

MIND TRICKS THAT MAKE LEARNING A PIECE OF CAKE

DISCOVER:

- **Ride memory waves to study less and remember more**

- **Know what not to study**

- **Ringing bells, salivating dogs, and the power of triggers**

- **Music: if it's not baroque, fix it**

- **Quit often**

- **Ways to train yourself for relaxed concentration**

RIDE MEMORY WAVES TO STUDY LESS AND RETAIN MORE

Although it might seem that some of the material you hear at school goes in one ear and out the other, ten minutes after you've learned something your memory of that newly acquired information peaks.

Yes, that's right. Ten minutes after you've learned something, your brain has had the opportunity to integrate what you've learned with the information already stored there.

Your job is to make the most of that powerful pocket of time about five to ten minutes after class. As soon as you leave a class, review—if only for a few moments—what you've just covered. And boom! In a tiny investment of time, you have already begun to give those newly learned concepts a solid place in your mind.

Now, you'll need to review again, of course. The next time you'll want to make sure you look at this new material is 24 hours later. Revisit it after no longer than a week, and again no longer than a month later, and again after 4 months.

According to Tony Buzan, author of *Make the Most of Your Mind*, this "organized series of special times" will allow the information to enter long-term memory. That's where all the firmly ingrained information, such as our address and phone number, is stored. Once safely in long-term memory, these facts and figures can be retrieved for automatic recall.

KNOW WHAT NOT TO STUDY

Everything. Don't study everything, that is. Don't reread the entire book. No need to read *every* note if you've written them in long hand. You should have periodically reduced those notes to key concepts and greatly reduced their bulk. Don't go back and painstakingly try to recreate the entire term thus far. The more important issue is to review the main concepts, key words, and their connections.

Why? Info overload, my friend. You have to help your brain out, here. Your mind works best at integrating key concepts when it connects it to others it has stored already. It takes the new ideas and associates them through comparison and contrast with the other knowledge you have stored in long-term memory.

> While it may seem like a real sacrifice and a good idea to force yourself to study late at night after a full day of work, family responsibilities, and possibly even an evening class, DO NOT study late at night if you are mentally tapped out.
>
> If you are so tired you literally can't think straight, don't think that you will get anything out of your study session. Best to get a good night's rest and get up a half hour early than to spend three times that long pushing yourself beyond your limit when you won't remember any of it in the morning, anyway.

As brilliant as your potential is, there is no need to overtax your brain by trying to incorporate every single thought uttered by the professor or written in your text. It's simple overkill. It's also extra work, by the way. So remember Einstein's idea of "optimal simplicity" and keep everything as simple as possible (and no simpler).

RINGING BELLS, SALIVATING DOGS, AND THE POWER OF TRIGGERS

Remember Ivan Pavlov? He was the scientist who studied the link among a ringing bell, dogs, dinner, and dogs' salivation. (Ick! I know, but hear me out). So there's Pavlov, ringing the bell, and giving the dogs dinner, ringing the bell, and giving the dogs dinner. Of course, when the dogs got their dinner, what would they do? Salivate, that's right.

Pavlov found out that after enough times of linking the ringing bells to receiving food, these dogs would only need to hear the bell and they'd start salivating as though food were right there in front of them. The "Pavlovian response" refers to the connection between one stimulus (the ringing bell) and a previously unassociated reaction. (That is, until the dogs learned to associate the ringing bell with food, they wouldn't salivate just because a bell rang within earshot.)

So what does this have to do with you and that History final? You can start creating your own Pavlovian response.

Imagine this: You have only a couple of places you regularly study, your dining table, at your desk during lunch. You go there, take out your study materials, take out your thermos of coffee, tea, or soda, scoot your chair in, open your notebook and textbook and start reviewing. Same place, same process, every time.

When you go through this little ritual, you follow the exact same steps every time. Those series of movements actually gear you up to prepare to study. Your brain quickly catches on that this ritual signals study time.

According to Edward de Bono, a pioneer in helping people learn how to think, your subconscious will read your body language, including your posture, as a signal that it's time to start some learning. So sit up, and your subconscious will take note.

You are using the powerful mind/body connection to associate this series of movements with taking in and learning new information. This is also called "state dependent learning," by the way. It means you're creating the same conditions time and again and will get the same results. You sit down at a table and an upright chair, pull out your History text and notes, and a flood of memories about what you've learned in class so far easily makes it way to your ready recall.

By the way, if you are sitting up in a chair, at a desk, this arrangement is very much like what you'll experience in the testing environment, isn't it? You are further preparing yourself for performing well when you take the test because you have assimilated the information in the same manner in which you'll be expected to recall it. This also enhances memory.

Pretty neat trick, isn't it?

MUSIC: IF IT'S NOT BAROQUE, FIX IT

First, my apologies for the cheesy joke. I'm writing this section while burning the midnight oil myself (something you will soon relate to, if you don't already.) Apparently, sometimes my humor retires before I do.

Meanwhile, back to our musical solution.

Listen to music, by all means, plug in, put the earphones on, and crank it up. If, that is, it's a certain type of baroque, specifically, the kind that is sixty beats a minute. (Know what else is sixty beats per minute? That's right—the average heart rate!)

Dr. Georgi Lozanov was a Bulgarian educator who specialized in accelerated learning techniques. He found that baroque music makes learning quicker and easier. In their book, *Quantum Learning: Unleashing the Genius in You,* Bobbi DePorter and Mike Hernacki note that Bach, Handel, Pachelbel, and Vivaldi (composers of the kind of music that will facilitate learning) "used very specific beats and patterns that automatically synchronize our minds with our bodies." DePorter and Hernacki also note that this kind of music allows the highly logical part of your brain to incorporate the new material.

By the way, taking a foreign language class? Dr. Lozanov's studies of listening to baroque during learning made a tremendous difference in the number of foreign words a student was able to learn.

Are you supposed to go out and buy these baroque CDs? Sure, if you like. Or, you can do what I did. Go to your library and check out anything by Bach, Handel, Pachelbel, and Vivaldi. My resource librarian showed me exactly where these gems are kept. Once I got a feel for what I liked, I went out and bought a few of my own. I often listen now when I'm writing, and when I'm doing something that requires higher levels of thought, like balancing my checkbook each month.

One more thing: using baroque music when you study adds another aspect to the study "ritual" and helps you associate this with study and learning time.

So tune in and turn it up a bit. It's good for you!

While I recommend the kind of music I've mentioned here, it's also possible that you can listen to other kinds of music and prepare your mind for thoughtful studying. Note that I do NOT recommend any kind of music with lyrics as it's too distracting. Also, make it the background noise and keep it low or you'll distract yourself and defeat your purpose.

QUIT OFTEN

We remember the first and last things studied.

Make sure you don't confuse the information you've stored in intermediate memory with that which is solidly stored in long-term memory.

According to research, intermediate memory lasts only about 4 to 8 hours. So, when you go to the movies, you can remember where you parked your car a few hours later (well, usually!) yet, you don't store that for ready recall the next time when you park somewhere else.

Sometimes, novice college students will sit down to an afternoon of studying, get really determined and decide they will only take one bathroom break halfway through a four-hour session.

No, no, no. Not only are feats of prolonged study not necessary, they have a negative effect.

Your brain needs to an opportunity to process all of this information. As naturally brilliant as you are, you still have to cut your mind some slack and let it connect the new knowledge with the old knowledge. Give it an opportunity to give it meaning and context. This takes a few minutes. Not many, only about five or ten.

Be sure to schedule a break at least every 50 minutes for relatively easy material. If it's more challenging, schedule a shorter break every 15 minutes or so.

WAYS TO TRAIN YOURSELF FOR RELAXED CONCENTRATION

It can be done, you can actually train yourself to deeply relax and maintain concentration for long periods of time.

Have you heard of being in the "flow?" It's when you're so engrossed and challenged by rewarding work that you have no concept of time passing by. It's a great feeling, isn't it?

You can get in the flow where you're studying and the time you spend under the condition of relaxed concentration will exponentially surpass any time you could have spent trying to multitask as you studied, or being distract by the demands of the "real world" when you sat down to hit the books.

Here's the quick version of how to do this.

First, get to the quietest place you can find. I can relate if that's a challenge for you. I have three kids myself!

Second, sit or lie down and close your eyes.

Then, breathe deeply, in through the nose, and imagine you're filling your lungs from the bottom up.

Breathe in to the count of seven.

Hold for eight counts.

Exhale for seven counts.

Repeat twice.

Go through your body by left and right legs, torso, chest, left and

50   © Crystal Jonas

right arms and, finally, head.

As you imagine each body part, say it's getting warm and heavy. Then say it's completely warm and heavy. Then move on to the next body part.

Next, imagine a cool cloth is over your forehead, it's the only cool part of your body.

Now, imagine that you are releasing all of the tension in your face. (Amazing, isn't in, how much tension we carry in our faces!)

REST AREA

Such conditioning is fast and profoundly effective for preparing yourself for academic success and being able to stay relaxed and concentrating on the task at hand. You will be amazed and delighted with how you can train your brain to perform at higher and higher levels of efficiency. The more you practice, the better you'll become.

After you feel relaxed, talk yourself through the vision you have of yourself proudly walking across that stage at the completion of your college program. You are getting your degree and those who love you most are there in the audience so proud of you. Feel the diploma in your hand and feel the pride and satisfaction of having accomplished this tremendous goal.

Walk yourself back in time, mentally as you imagine you've just finished the semester you're in now. See yourself getting your report card and you have wonderful grades. Digress a little more to the point where you see yourself getting back each quiz, test, and paper. You've done beautifully on all of your work.

Again, digress as you imagine (with great clarity) yourself about to sit down to study that very subject you were just imagining. You open your notebook and textbook, and it all starts to come together. Everything clicks as you study. You have clarity, understanding, and an uncanny ability to recall everything you want to.

When you are ready, slowly open your eyes and open your book.

You'll find that the more you walk through this exercise, the easier it gets to go through the images quickly.

Congratulations!

You're entitled to receive FREE Special Report excerpted from Crystal's CD album, *More Goodies, Less Effort* on Personal and Professional Success.

You'll find details in:
College Success Tips
And
Career Success Tips

Sign up for one or both of these FREE weekly tips by logging on to www.crystaljonas.com.

With these tips, you'll be able to:
• Breeze through college
• Have companies looking for you
• Cultivate social skills others admire
• Lead people
• Land the dream job and move quickly up
• Work less and have more to show for it

Go to www.CrystalJonas.comand sign up now. You'll be glad you did.

Learn more about how to get Crystal's CD album, *More Goodies, Less Effort*, by sending an e-mail to Crystal@CrystalJonas.com with the subject: CD album.

CHAPTER 6

THINK OUTSIDE THE BOOKS:

NONTRADITIONAL SOLUTIONS FOR NONTRADITIONAL STUDENTS

DISCOVER:

- **Special advantages of the Nontraditional Student (NT)**

- **Resources just for you**

- **Exciting news about brain power as you age**

- **Recognize opportunities to pull ahead**

- **How to focus on demand**

SPECIAL ADVANTAGES OF NONTRADITIONAL STUDENTS

Can a mild-mannered, well-meaning, hard-working full-fledged adult carry on all of the responsibilities and demands of work, school, and home and still maintain some semblance of sanity?

Glad you asked—and of course you can! Not only do you have absolutely everything it takes to do well in school, non-traditional students ("NTs" is a term institutions of higher learning use for students 25 years old or better) do every bit as well as their younger counterparts. In some areas, they do even better than the younger students on campus.

Of course, successfully continuing your education takes some work on your part, just like any other worthy accomplishment. With some guidance on how to use the resources you already have at your disposal, and your determination to see yourself as a college graduate, you will find yourself walking across the stage to collect that well-earned diploma before you know it.

You have a distinct advantage in going back to school now. You fully appreciate what education can do for you. Perhaps you have seen others younger than you with much less experience in your industry come in and be promoted over you simply because they had earned their college degree. Maybe you tried college years ago, then married and started your family, dropping out of school to take care of your many responsibilities. It could be that back then, you just weren't ready yet, and didn't do your best.

Trust me when I tell you that NTs tend to do very well in school because they appreciate what it can do for them and they have all kinds of internal motivation to see their formal education through to completion.

RESOURCES JUST FOR YOU

A major concern that some NTs have is whether they'll remember enough from the "olden days" of high school. Some are really concerned because they've been down this path before and weren't such stellar students the first time around.

It doesn't matter how much your past may have hindered your success, my friend. Whatever your concern, your college of choice has seen the worst of it and has a plan for helping out any student who sincerely wants to go back to and successfully complete school. If the school has accepted you, rest assured that they have a system in place to help you be successful.

More people over 24 than ever are returning to college. They are only slightly less than half of the student body. In fact, NT numbers are so large on campuses across the country that many have advisors and special perks and programs that are designed specifically to cater to NTs. Many schools even have academic advisors that only work with NTs. So, you're in good hands and at the right place.

Your first act should be to find out what kind of support the school you are considering offers its NTs. See if they have special financial and academic advisors. Find out if there is a day care facility for your young ones to be close by while you're in class. Inquire about placement tests that can help you figure out what classes you should be taking. Ask about any special preparatory classes you might want to take, and look into tutoring that might be available just for NTs.

EXCITING NEWS ABOUT BRAIN POWER AS YOU AGE

Back when most NTs were in school, people still believed that the brain lost copious amounts of brain cells throughout life and that this would gradually wear away a person's ability to learn and remember. In fact, we used to believe that a poor memory was an inevitable result of getting older.

And now, fortunately, we know better.

Have you heard that we use about 10% of our brainpower? Current research now reflects we use about 1%. In fact, the more we learn about this "sleeping giant" the less of it researchers tell us we're using.

See, we all have about 10 billion neurons (or brain cells). Yes, that's billion with a "b." Each of these neurons communicates with those around it through connections called dendrites. You can grow more dendrites as you age. Now, I've obviously greatly simplified the complex workings of the most powerful "computer" in the universe.

The point is this: your brain can continue to understand, remember, and recall on demand new ideas as long as you continue to "exercise" it. The more you learn, the more you can learn. So, as you age and add to your mental stores, you can add even more knowledge.

I can almost hear the question running through your head right now: "Yes, but how do I exercise my brain?"

Good question!

You exercise your brain by using it. Memory works by connecting new thoughts to the ideas that you've already stored in your memory. The more you know, the easier it is to learn more. This is because you have more associations to make with the new material.

It's astoundingly simple how complex it all is. Or, is it astoundingly complex how simple it all is?

The bottom line is this, the more you continue to read, and play games that allow you to use your mind, and interact with people and engage in lively conversation, the more you will find learning even more new stuff to be easier than you ever imagined.

See, all of the life experience that you have had up to this point has really only kept your mind limber and prepared you to go out and quickly learn new material. You are that much more ahead of all those younger students who'll be in your classes with you.

Sort of makes you feel a whole lot more confident about this whole going back to school prospect, doesn't it?

Your experiences and ability to make the most of your mental muscle, as well as a staunch inward drive to succeed in college add up to quite a powerful academic advantage.

RECOGNIZE THESE OPPORTUNITIES TO PULL AHEAD

A simple bittersweet rule of life: there is never going to be enough time to do all of the things we want to do. All our lives we will be faced with decisions of how to spend our time—all the time knowing that in the very act of choosing one thing, we turn away other possibilities.

Knowing exactly what you want and wanting it with every fiber of your being will allow you to make decisions about how you will spend time much easier.

The trick is to find moments in each day for which you have nothing planned, and be prepared to use them. Notice all the times during the week when you're standing in line, or waiting for someone, or have no control over the fact that you have to wait until the next event in your busy schedule begins. Use these pockets of time wisely.

Think of these moments in which you have nothing you must do as gifts of time, and be ready to mentally rehearse some of this won-

MINIMUM SPEED LIMIT

Minimum
Speed
Limit
45

As a minimum, you need to replace some of the time you used to spend watching TV with study sessions. While it may be too much of a radical lifestyle change to wipe out all of your TV habits, you need to be conscious of how much time you spend in front of the tube.

Write the time down whenever you sit in a room with a TV that's turned on. Log when you leave the room or when the TV goes off. You'll be amazed at how quickly time flies when you're in a room with a TV that's turned on. Whether you're actively watching or not, you will be subconsciously distracted by it.

Bottom line about this whole TV thing: Consciously choose to watch those shows you really enjoy, and make them a reward for time spent involved in schoolwork. Reduce your usual TV time by at least half.

derful new knowledge you've been taking in.

You realize that your free time is scarce and a precious commodity. The gift of pockets of time will serve you well in squeezing in chances to read, study, and review.

Think for a moment about all of the times you spend waiting. It could be in a grocery line, at the bank, doctor's office, on the commuter train, at the office before a meeting starts, or waiting for your kid's soccer practice to be over.

You're likely to spend a measurable amount of time every day with your schedule at someone else's mercy. Use these spaces below to write down some of those times when you know you'll spend five or more minutes waiting:

_____

_____

_____

_____

_____

Now, start thinking of what you can do to read, review, or somehow plan your next assignment for school. You could, for example, write down your vocabulary words for your French class and carry those 3" x 5" index cards in your pocket for when you run errands and you expect to be waiting in more than one line. You could carry your history notebook to your daughter's dance class and test yourself to see how much material you can recall without looking at your book. You could take your psychology textbook to work so you can spend half of every lunch hour reading a portion of your assignment.

In the spaces below, write down how you might use these golden nuggets of time:

_____

_____

_____

_____

_____

CUT YOURSELF SOME SLACK

Nontraditional students are much more likely to be much too hard on themselves when it comes to doing well in school. By all means, set your standards high. You are certainly making some big sacrifices here and you want maximum return on your investment.

Returning to school can have other rewards. Many find that they enjoy the social connections, the intellectual simulation, and the personal satisfaction from going back to school.

I hear from thousands of adult college students from across the world who write to me through my website at www.crystaljonas.com. There are a small but significant number of e-mails from returning students who are full of concern and quite a bit of stress. It's interesting to me that they all use the same kind of words to describe their challenges. These e-mails tend to include the words:

"should"

"ought to"

"must"

"have to"

That's a whole lot of life out of control when you describe your situation with those words.

I loudly applaud your decision to return to school. Good for you. No, GREAT for you! Let's change the way you talk to yourself about the whole experience though, shall we? Change your language and self-talk, and I guarantee you, you will change your state of mind and give your outlook a much-needed makeover.

Instead of feeling that you have no other choice but to return to school, look at it for what it is: A choice that you are making of your own free will to improve your own station in life. Adopt these words in place of those on the list above:

"choose to"

"get to"

"want to"

"prefer"

Countless studies over hundreds of years have reaffirmed our abilities to profoundly influence our condition in life by what we say and think about all day.

HOW TO FOCUS ON DEMAND

How valuable would it be to you to be able to sit down and focus your attention completely on the task at hand whenever you needed to? You'd save yourself a ton of time and a load of aggravation, wouldn't you?

You can teach yourself to focus on demand. Try these simple steps:

Remove as many distractions as you can. (No one is forcing you to study in front of the TV just because that's where the rest of the family is. You're much better off getting 30 minutes of focused time on schoolwork than to sit with your book in your lap for three hours in front of the television.)

Use earplugs if outside sounds distract you. You can get them for next to nothing at your local drugstore.

Make a plan. Know exactly what you'll start with and how long you'll spend on it. For example:

- 30 minutes on Internet researching the French Revolution for History paper. (Then plan a 3 to 5 minute break.)
- 20 minutes reviewing Biology notes. Rewrite with key concepts only. (Short break)
- 10 minutes to brainstorm for term paper topic for English
- 15 minutes to review Literature notes (Short break)
- 10 minutes to revisit term paper ideas for English

Knowing exactly what you're going to study, for how long, and planning and sticking to breaks will keep your mind on a laser-sharp focus. At any time when your mind wanders, and be kind to yourself when it inevitably does, simply get right back into the schedule. You'll notice you don't need a big chunk of time at one time to get and stay focused.

The primary trick about staying focused on whatever you're doing is to have a clear purpose and a well-defined schedule.

You will amaze and delight yourself with how much you can accomplish in so little time when you put this process to work in your own life. It not only is effective with schoolwork, it works when you have projects you need to complete at your job too!

CHAPTER 7

LAUNCH A GREAT CAREER WHILE STILL IN SCHOOL

DISCOVER:

- How to set yourself up for your dream job

- The huge mistake most college seniors make that you must avoid

- The ideal time to begin your job search

- How to get people to recommend you for the best jobs

- Three powerful payoffs for networking, and how to do it right

- Bonus way to make the most of networking

- Resumes that attract the best job offers

- Anchors aweigh; studying across the pond

- Top two inexpensive, indispensable job search tools

HOW TO SET YOURSELF UP FOR YOUR DREAM JOB

To get more goodies, you've got to go beyond the books.

Making the most of college means more than finishing—or even finishing with great grades. Some people center the entire focus of their years in higher education on walking across the stage in cap and gown and collecting a firm handshake and a sheepskin. For them, success will mean only getting the degree.

Sad, when you think of how much more they could have had if only they had dreamed bigger and gone for more. They could have had created for themselves life-long friendships, career-making experiences, and grand memories. Rich opportunities await those willing to open up their eyes, ears, hearts, and minds to the possibilities that lie in maximizing the college experience. This book is dedicated to helping you do just that.

SCENIC ROUTE

To get the best bang for your buck from your major investment of time, money, and mental muscle, you should start with a plan of just what you want to achieve while you're at "The Big U." Be sure to include the FUN things you want to do, like join some clubs that have nothing to do with academics. Try out lots of activities and meetings, and then stick with a few that you really enjoy. You'll never have so many opportunities at your fingertips as you do when you're in school.

Life is like an all-you-can-eat buffet

Some people go with the idea that they can only have a little at life's buffet (maybe they're on a diet and they are stuck in this limiting frame of mind). Some people go and get what they always get, because it's safe, and they don't want to try anything new, even though they can always return to the old standby if the new things don't work for them.

And some people have the adventurous spirit of daring to try new things, to taste it all, and go back for more, enjoying the process.

You see, there is plenty there and plenty more. You are only limited by your desire and willingness to take action and step up to partake.

A smorgasbord of choices at your fingertips

College offers so many opportunities in the areas of academics, sports, clubs, social, religious, and professional organizations, volunteering, leadership, career development and advancement (and more!), that your greatest challenge lies in choosing just what you want to emphasize during your fun-filled, life-expanding years at school.

You see, you can do anything; you just won't have enough time in a day to do everything. I talk with thousands of students all over the country, and focusing on too much at once ends up backfiring big time.

When you divide your attention among too many activities, you end up not doing well in any of them. Remember, when everything is important, nothing is important.

Although the world is your oyster while you're in school, and you will never (and I do mean never) have the same wealth of choices in the real world, you'll need to quickly develop laser-guided focus on those goals that mean the most to you.

THE MISTAKE MOST SENIORS MAKE THAT YOU MUST AVOID

Whatever your career search strategy, be sure you don't fall into the trap that far too many seniors do. Sometime around the last round of midterms, they start putting together their resumes and mass mailing them out to every company within a 100-mile radius of where they'd like to live. Often that's the same town where they're going to school.

Make sure you don't follow in their misguided footsteps.

Picture it. It's about six weeks before graduation, and suddenly, every big company within commuting distance of the university gets a flood of resumes from soon-to-be graduates. Not exactly the ideal strategy for setting yourself apart from the crowd.

THE IDEAL TIME TO BEGIN YOUR JOB SEARCH

There's an ancient Chinese saying: "The best time to plant a tree was 20 years ago. The second best time is today."

The ideal time to begin your job search was as soon as you

discovered what field you wanted to study at college.

The second best ideal time is this moment.

And you have plenty of time. Just make sure you do begin now.

Whatever your class year right at this moment, start making decisions about how you'll spend the rest of your college career based on what kind of work you'd like to do after you graduate.

Be bold. Don't let anyone's impression of what's possible hold you back. As long as you're willing to continually put the effort into entering the career field of your dreams, you have as much chance as anyone to make your ideal career your own.

Here's your key: Plan now. Start getting into classes and extra-curricular activities that will allow you to begin networking with faculty, staff, and fellow students who can help you make the connections necessary to get your foot in the door with internships or job studies. The more you build relationships and develop job experience in the area in which you're interested, the more likely you are to stand above the crowd of all of those other college students trying to get the same job you are.

Just make sure you do this as soon as possible, so that in December of your senior year, you have already begun sending out those resumes and calling and writing your contacts to respectfully ask for recommendations.

Many students with vision and a clear plan receive attractive job offers as early as halfway through their senior year (and earlier in some career fields!) and have made their choice before they graduate.

Imagine how gratified (not to mention relieved) you'll feel to have a great job waiting for you when you graduate!

HOW TO GET PEOPLE TO RECOMMEND YOU FOR THE BEST JOBS

Stand on the shoulders of giants; get a mentor

While you're in school, you are surrounded by dozens, possibly hundreds, of people who could help you if you cultivate professional relationships with them and ask for their help. By building rapport with your professors, and those you meet through being involved in school, and going out of your way to meet the distinguished guests that visit colleges and universities, you have opportunities that you may never have again to make professional connections.

What you may not realize at this point is that many of your school's professors are very well connected. They know a lot of people in businesses and industries who need hardworking, smart people just like you. They may even have strong political connections, and may know people in power who live on the other side of the country, or even on another continent.

I know you've heard the cliché "don't reinvent the wheel." That absolutely applies here. Don't waste your time, energy, and money making mistakes when there are plenty of people who would be quite willing to help you if you just let them know you would appreciate their input. Most successful business people appreciate the importance of learning from other successful people, and many have themselves benefited from having mentors.

THE EASIEST WAY TO GET HELP FINDING A GREAT JOB

It's human nature to want to share information with others. When someone asks your opinion about a movie that just came out, or the best place to call for pizza delivery, aren't you happy to help out? If someone asked you to tell your story about how you did something well, wouldn't you welcome the chance to share your story? Of course.

The same goes for professors. They are happy to help out and connect any diligent student with a great attitude who wants their help and asks for it.

The easiest way to get help finding a great job is simply to ask for it! And the best thing about asking for help is that you get so much high quality help, just by asking. At school, you're in the perfect situation for meeting smart, well-connected people who, for the most part, genuinely enjoy helping people.

That's help that is hard to come by outside of school. Be sure to make the most of it.

HOW TO GET A MENTOR

Start out slowly. Make an appointment with a professor you like and feel comfortable with and find out if you could talk with him about your ideas to follow in whatever career path you'd like to pursue. Of course, you are the kind of student who always comes on time to class and stays the entire time. It's bad form to be asking favors of someone you've shown disrespect to by skipping his class.

What do you think of his feedback and information? Was it useful? Did he listen well? Did he ask you questions to find out what your personal interests are so he could better advise you?

If you and he are getting along well and you're finding his advice helpful, continue to get on his schedule and meet with him from time to time. You need to make sure that you follow through on all pieces of advice that are useful to you. Also make sure you let him know how the advice worked for you. This follow up advice is a crucial part of the equation that most novice networkers neglect. **Make sure you don't make that mistake.**

For example, let's say your professor gave you the name and number of a high-ranking person he knows in an industry you might be interested in. He gets you in the door to see this industry leader and you go to meet her.

Follow up with your mentor and let him know that you met with his contact on whatever date and time, and that you learned so much.

Be sure to:

- Write a thank you note to both your professor who gave you the contact information, and the person who agreed to meet with you.
- Write the thank you note on the same day as the meeting and get it in the mail that night. Do this immediately for two reasons:
  1. It's something almost no one else is thoughtful enough to do, especially right away.
  2. If you don't take care of your notes right away, you'll forget and end up not writing them.

And you will become like all of the other people who are smart enough to know they are supposed to network, yet not persistent enough to follow up immediately. In other words, in following up quickly, you will look good where few people do.

Mention a comment made by the person you just met, so that she knows she did something very specific to help you out. It also shows that you were listening. Let your professor know what you gathered

MINIMUM SPEED LIMIT

The least you can do is to write thank you notes when someone takes the time to cash in "brownie points" to get you face time with a well-connected person. Write a note to that contact, and the person who connected you letting the "connector" know how well the meeting went.

Send the note snail mail. How will you know this new person's address? Simple, ask for a business card and ask if you may keep in touch.

Do this, and you will distinguish yourself far ahead of the pack!

from the meeting as well.

Don't think you need to restrict yourself to only one mentor. You can have one for each area of your life you want to work on. You may find that you want mentors to help you develop spiritually, academically, professionally, and even financially!

THREE POWERFUL PAYOFFS FOR NETWORKING, AND HOW TO DO IT RIGHT

For a while, networking had taken a bum rap because some mistaken people thought that it was all about what someone else could do for them.

When you network and start expanding your social and professional circle, always be thinking: "What can I do for this person?"

Networking is important for three main reasons:

1. Relationships are what matters most in this world. In the very end, the things that you will remember and that which is priceless are your connections to other people.

2. The more people you know, the smarter you are. Samuel Johnson said there are two kinds of knowledge: our own knowledge of a subject, and knowledge we have by knowing who knows. You don't have to know everything, and you know a lot more when you know someone to whom you can go when you need more information.

3. Have you heard the saying, "It's not what you know, it's who you know?" Well, that's true to an extent. As mentioned in #2, the more people you know, the broader your knowledge base. Here's a twist on that: "It's not who you know, it's who knows you." Makes you think, doesn't it?

   Always be "who you are, at your best." There is always someone watching you and noticing you. Be at your best, and people will hear about you. Don't, and they still will.

BONUS WAY TO MAKE THE MOST OF NETWORKING

Stay in touch. Many people are starting to catch on that networking means touching base with new people they've met. Where they drop the ball is that they don't stay connected.

How often do you get in contact, and what do you do to maintain this connection?

A good rule of thumb is to contact that new friend once every two to three months. Not very often, is it? Is it starting to sound like something you'd be willing to do? I hope so, because I know for a fact it will make a difference for you.

What can you do to stay connected?

If you know their birthday, send them a card when it approaches. Know their hobbies and interests so you can send an article from a professional journal, a website they might enjoy, a cartoon (if it's rated G, of course), a book review, or information about a speaker coming to their neighborhood. Pretty easy stuff, wouldn't you say?

The point is, just keep the link. Be friendly, upbeat, and brief.

RESUMES THAT ATTRACT THE BEST JOB OFFERS

Make that resume more interesting and compelling to potential employers.

Let's face facts. Lots of college students graduate with a good GPA. Those "A's" and "B's" are especially important if you're looking to go to graduate school, but alone, they aren't usually enough to have employers beating down your door to offer you the corner office.

Add other elements to make your resume (and you!) stand apart from the rest of the crowd.

While you're at school, you have *more opportunities than you will ever again have in your life* to meet hundreds of diverse people and to experience a wide variety of activities that extend beyond school.

Clubs and various organizations on your campus will fling open the doors of opportunity for you.

Not only will you have countless chances to take part in wide range of activities, you will build an impressive resume by taking an active part in a few well-chosen clubs.

My suggestion is that you include a variety of associations. You'll find professional associations, as well as volunteer opportunities, and athletic and religious groups. Pick what you most enjoy, and be actively involved. Take on a leadership position in at least one club. And track your contributions of time and physical labor.

For example, if you worked with Habitat for Humanity, you'll want to quantify how many hours you contributed and where the work was done. Best to get a thank you letter from the person involved in organizing the project. And how do you get a thank you letter? That's right, you ask for it.

When you receive a compliment (and you will) say, "Thank you, I've really enjoyed working with this group. Your words mean a lot to me, and I'd love you have you as a reference as I conduct my job search. May I get a letter from you with a few brief comments about the work I've done for Habit for Humanity this summer?"

Of course, the person you're asking will say yes. Now, make it easy for them to say something nice and specific by jotting down a few notes that they can include in their letter. Your notes can include how many hours you've spent on the project and the results from your work. Feel free to include nice comments that others have said to you. Be sure to write down their names, and when you receive a compliment, be sure to ask, "May I quote you?"

When you get the letter, write a thank you note. And when you land your dream job, write a note to everyone who helped you along the way. Continue to stay connected. And continue to think of ways you can be of service to them.

ANCHORS AWEIGH; STUDYING ACROSS THE POND

Add a huge mark in your favor by studying abroad. It's quite an impressive addition to your resume to have gone to another country to study.

There are some assumptions made about people who leave the comfort of their own country to go overseas for a semester. Now, perhaps some of these generalizations are inaccurate. However, let me list a few, and ask yourself if these are fair enough assumptions:

Studying abroad suggests you have:

- Initiative
- Willingness to take calculated risks
- Courage
- Persistence
- Self-leadership
- Tolerance of other cultures
- Intellectual curiosity
- Spirit of adventure

Look down the list. A person who possesses these qualities is destined for the fast track. It will never hurt, and will likely serve you well if you do invest the time, money, and mental energy studying in a foreign country.

The networking opportunity 99% of your classmates will blow off

Occasionally, you will have the opportunity to hear guest speakers who are leading experts in their fields. Some schools have a big, fat budget and can really get some heavy hitters as guest speakers. Be sure to stay after, and meet these people, even if you have to stand in line. Write them a personal note afterwards telling them how much you enjoyed their talk. Be sure to mention a particular point that caught your attention, so they know you were listening, and you're not just writing a generic note. Once every eight weeks or so, drop them a few lines in a personal note. You can include an article you think they might be interested in.

Keep their card in your contact system, whether it's a hardcopy system, or a computer program. The point is that it's not too soon to start a file on contacts. In fact, the sooner you start, the longer you have to build professional relationships with people before you get to graduation and start looking for a job.

Stay in touch with your contact base, connecting with each person about once every eight to twelve weeks. You don't need to go to some big, expensive school to have the opportunity to meet and stay in touch with leading experts in your field. When you like the speaker's message, always take the opportunity to network with that person.

TOP TWO INEXPENSIVE, INDISPENSABLE JOB SEARCH TOOLS

As you build your resume while in school, be sure that you track your accomplishments as you go.

Do not, under any circumstance, rely on memory to keep this straight. You have far too much going on to be expected to remember all of your achievements and contacts.

One tool you must have is a log that tracks your accomplishments, and involvement in clubs and various activities. Keep all letters of appreciation and certificate in this log.

The second tool you'll need is a log so you can track your contacts. You can use the same log or you can use contact software. You will also want to know what you send to your contacts each time so you can vary how and when you stay in contact. For example, if you sent a cartoon they might like in one letter, you don't want to send another cartoon the very next time to the same person.

If you follow even some of the ideas in this chapter you will begin to pull ahead of the pack of the hundreds of people who apply for the job you want. Take every positive action you can to set yourself apart from the hordes that are competing for your job.

And start right away! There are many things you can do while still in college to jumpstart you career.

Always remember that you have exactly what it takes to make this a richly rewarding adventure.

CHAPTER 8

TAKE THE FAST TRACK TO PROFESSIONAL SUCCESS

DISCOVER:

- **How to get no-pressure, high visibility job interviews**

- **The precise way to ask for what you want**

- **Qualities of people who get promoted quickly**

- **The talent companies hire for**

- **Where most people fail**

- **Ways to control concentration and physical intensity**

HOW TO GET NO-PRESSURE, HIGH-VISIBILITY INTERVIEWS

You have choices. You can start your career search as a one-of-hundreds, anonymous face in the crowd each one competing for a minimal paying, entry-level job. Or, you can get out there, make maximum contacts, and meet and impress people much higher up the organizational food chain who have the power to put you in a position that may even be above that entry-level job.

To make maximum contact and to get in front of those upper level decision makers, go on "information interviews."

These are shockingly simple to get. All you have to do is start with one well-connected contact with whom you've established rapport. (In other words, you two have to respect each other. No fair hitting up someone for favors if you haven't established a connection with him or her yet. People you want to recommend you need to know you're a decent person before giving you the private office number of their good friend.)

THE PRECISE WAY TO ASK FOR WHAT YOU WANT

Ask who they know who might be able to tell you more about the industry you're interested in. Notice how that question is phrased. Say, "Professor Finkeldink, I'm thinking of becoming a playwright. Who do you know in the entertainment industry that might be willing to let me interview them on what it takes to be successful in that career?" Ask, "Who do you know?" It has a powerful way of evoking the answers that you want, unlike the question, "Do you know anyone?" That's a poorly worded question because it usually gets a knee-jerk response of "No."

Once you get this contact's information. Call and say, "Ms. Aardvark, I'm a student at (wherever) and I'm studying to be a script writer. Professor Finkeldink mentioned you might be willing to talk with me for a few minutes about what it takes to be a successful playwright. Would you perhaps have 20 minutes this week when we could meet? I realize you're very busy, and I am happy to meet with you wherever and whenever it's convenient for you." By this time, your contact will say something like "Well, how is Sparky Finkeldink?" or something along those lines. And you spend a bit of time saying something nice, of course.

Chances are quite good that this person will grant you an interview. Your purpose in this information interview is to find out what it takes to be successful. Come prepared with the questions you want to ask, be on time, take a few notes, and leave after the agreed time has passed. Do not wear out your welcome!

Some questions you may want to ask:

- How did you get started in this career field?
- What do you love most about it?
- What are the drawbacks in this industry?
- Are there any professional associations for this career field?
- Are there any classes you recommend I take?
- If you had it to do again, what would you do differently?
- May I have your card and stay in touch with you occasionally?
- Who do you know that I can contact to find out more?
  (This should be something you've discovered as you've been listening and want to learn more about.)

STOP

Don't spin your wheels blindly mass mailing hundreds of unsolicited resumes. Make sure you're getting in front of people with the power to hire you, or at least to recommend you to the people who do the hiring.

The best way to get noticed by high-level people where you think you'd like to work is by getting an "information interview." You're just there to ask them how they got where they are today and what advice they might have for you. It's a super way to get noticed as a smart, career-focused person. Once you've established this contact, by all means, stay in touch.

For tips on how to maintain contact, go to the section of this book that covers networking.

Of all questions, the last is perhaps the most important and the beginning of casting what could be an enormous network web. In asking your new contact whom they know that you should talk with, you will probably get at least two names, and from interviewing those two, you'll get two or three more from each of them. You can see where your new network grows quickly.

When you ask for additional contacts, be sure to ask for their contact information, such as office phone numbers. Ask how they know that person, and if you may use their name.

Follow this process, and you will have many informative and completely low-pressure interviews. You'll get major face time with people quite high in the career field you're interested in. This is a very smart move on your part.

At the end, if you feel it is all going well, you may want to ask about any internships that might be available. Your interviewee might have such information. You will need to use your best people skills to evaluate if this will be well received. If the vibes are good, it couldn't hurt to ask. After all, you're not asking for a permanent, full time job, just for an internship possibility.

QUALITIES OF PEOPLE WHO GET PROMOTED QUICKLY

Bosses are looking to promote people who:
- Have a positive attitude
- Are team players
- Understand and support the organization's purpose
- Take well-considered initiative
- Plan and prioritize work
- Have leadership potential

THE TALENT COMPANIES HIRE FOR

Hiring professionals know that you hire for attitude first; you can always teach the necessary skills later.

How easy are you to get along with? Have you been told (by people who care about you) that you may need an attitude adjustment? If one nasty person from your past cut you down, don't let that hold you back. However, if you consistently hear that you've got some personality traits to work on, I do hope you'll ask someone you trust for suggestions on how to change those characteristics for the better.

MINIMUM SPEED LIMIT

Minimum Speed Limit 45	You're expected to get along with people, yet most people fail in this crucial skill. Research reflects that 85% if our success lies in our ability to get along with others.

THE GET ALONG FACTOR

Eventually, even if you work in an isolated cubicle where you hardly see another person, you will need to interact with others at work.

Those who rise to the top quickly can get along with a wide variety of personalities, regardless of how different they may be.

Practice tolerance and be easy going.

Being a good team player will be noticed and highly valued by your employer. Constant complainers who cannot work well with others drain time and energy from managers. They have a bad reputation throughout the organization, and are destined to stay stuck in a dead end job. Who would put them in a leadership position with that lousy attitude?

CLUED IN TO WHAT MATTERS MOST

Know what your employer is in business to do. What's their bottom line? Not all jobs are "for profit." What is your organization's mission?

You need to know this so that as you begin to learn your job and develop key skills necessary for success, you are focused on what really matters most to the company. Help them get more of what they want, and you will be truly valuable.

TAKE WELL-CONSIDERED INITIATIVE

People who rise quickly at work take initiative. They don't wait to be told what to do next. In fact, this is a key factor that distinguishes the managers who continue to rise in an organization to those who never go higher than middle management (at best).

Notice that the distinction is "well-considered" initiative. Always keep the organization's mission in mind when you are thinking of what you can add. Be thinking of ways you can help them get what they want.

WHERE MOST PEOPLE FAIL

You've got to plan and prioritize your work.

Many people are busy, yet few people are truly productive.

There is a "key skill" theory of excellence. The idea is that you only need to be good at a handful of key skills to be outstanding. Your job is to identify what those key skills are. How do you know what those are? Well, I'm mentioning a few in this list. Add to it any that are especially important in your chosen career field.

For example, if you want to be a salesperson for a pharmaceutical company, you will need to master advanced principles of persuasion in order to excel in that job.

So, plan your work based around what matters. Anything that falls out of the "key skill" area should quickly fall off your radar. You simply do not have enough hours in a day to pursue little tasks that don't add value to your company.

Every time you fill your time with busy work, you take away focus from developing those critical key skills.

OASIS

Don't become so busy being busy that you fail to notice if all that work is leading you where you want to go.

So many people fail because they confuse busy-ness with productivity. Just because you're always doing something, doesn't automatically mean you're doing the things you should be doing.

Your ability to know what's most important to the company, and to design your entire workload around doing what moves the company forward in its goals, are skills that separate you from the millions of other people who stay busy but have no clear concept of how their work benefits their company. And very often, the busy work that's so time consuming does not benefit the company.

Stay focused on what matters most and move quickly to the next important task. This is a strategy that will quickly boost you to the top of any organization.

HAVE LEADERSHIP POTENTIAL

Do you have the ability to see the talents of others and to inspire them to bring out those skills? This is a key quality of leadership.

Not many people can lead others, and those who do it well add a great deal of value to any organization.

You can cultivate leadership qualities by mastering the other six key skills on this list, and focusing on bringing out the best in others. Exceed expectations, and lead first by your own example.

Continue to work on self-growth. The best leaders are those that continue to work on being the very best themselves as they encourage others to use their unique talents to be at their best.

WAYS TO CONTROL CONCENTRATION AND PHYSICAL INTENSITY

Make sure you control your focus and intensity by keeping a clear eye on what you want and what it takes to get it. Then, be willing to be brutally honest with yourself to make sure that you are doing what needs to be done, when you need to do it.

There are plenty of ultra-busy, overworked people in this world. The question is, why exert so much effort without a clear understanding of how much energy is really needed to do only those activities that yield the best results?

Focus your energy and attention on your long and short-term goals. If what you are doing at any time isn't getting you what you want, stop doing it. Refocus your energy immediately.

WHAT FAILURE MEANS TO YOU

The only way to not make a single mistake is to not do anything!

As you grow in your career, exercise initiative, and take smart risks, you will make mistakes. Not a problem. As long as you are willing to learn from your mistakes, and get right back in the game, you're right on track.

Sadly, millions of talented people fail because they encounter challenges and give up. Yep, they pack it all in, say "It's too hard" or even "It can't be done." Why didn't they keep on going for their dreams? Well, for one thing, maybe they were never told that challenges and obstacles are natural detours on the success journey.

History is filled with countless examples of successful people who failed many times before they hit the big time. In fact, EVERYONE who has succeeded has run into troubles along the way. But they knew where they were going to end up. So, they picked themselves up, dusted themselves off, learned from the experience (Let's be blunt—it's fine to make a mistake, but it's pretty foolish not to learn from it.) and then they pressed on.

Thomas Edison said, "Many of life's failures are people who did not realize how close they were to success when they gave up."

Every day, do something to move yourself closer to what you want. Persist. Keep going. When you feel you couldn't possibly go even one more step, pick yourself up and move on anyway. Your richly deserved rewards lie right beyond that last challenge.

Your education is a gift you give yourself and one that will open doors of opportunity that would have otherwise stayed tightly closed. Refer to this book often. Pass it along to a friend when you're done. Better yet, get them their own as a gift.

Good luck in school and remember to enjoy your college journey!

CHAPTER 9

LIVING AN EXTRAORDINARY LIFE

DISCOVER:

- **Where all success starts**

- **The mindset that guarantees you'll win**

- **Fatal flaws of weak goals**

- **Seven sure steps for getting more goodies**

- **Magic moments in each day ideal for programming your mind for success**

- **The secret for overcoming the biggest barrier to goal achievement**

WHERE ALL SUCCESS STARTS

The college students I spoke to in Florida recently reminded me of how much they have in common with the business people I coach privately. Just about everyone I meet wants to be successful.

Unfortunately, few are willing to take the time to say exactly what it means to them to be successful.

OASIS

Wanting to be successful isn't clear enough to be considered a goal. Lily Tomlin uses a great line in her stand-up comedy routine: "All my life I wanted to be somebody. Now I see I should have been more specific."

If you want success to come to you, you need to get a handle on what the word means to you. Then you've got to create a plan to make it happen. And finally, you've got to hold yourself accountable for acting on the plan daily. In a nutshell, to be successful you've got to:

Define it; design it; do it.

Before you can have what you want, you've got to define exactly what it is you're going for. Next, write it down in great detail, and have a plan with deadlines for achieving what you want. Finally, work the plan daily. You will amaze yourself at where you will be in just a few months of following the success formula.

Colleges and corporations make *Living an Extraordinary Life*™ among the most popular programs I offer. Its goal lies in providing a step-by-step process for defining, designing, and realizing goals. Knowing the exact method for goal setting allows you to generate the kind of sustained persistence needed to bring about your goals.

To make college extraordinary and achieve uncommon results, you'll want to follow this proven and powerful process.

Dream big about what you want to get out of your investment of time and money in college, write down what you want to accomplish, and then work the plan with unflinching focus. I guarantee you that if you do this, you will exceed your own expectations.

"We are forever on the verge of all that is great. Trust in yourself;
claim your share of the greatness of life. Surrender yourself to the power
within you. Dare to become the master of your fate."

— *Ralph Waldo Emerson*

THE MINDSET THAT GUARANTEES YOU'LL WIN

You don't have to be a brain to be successful. Millions of socially, financially, and athletically successful people have proven this.

EXPRESSWAY

> **Expressway**
> **4.0**
>
> The starting point for all success begins right between your ears. You can be, do, and have anything you want if you are willing to change the way you see yourself.

The mindset that guarantees you will win what you want in this world is to believe that you can win. Carry that mindset with you and be willing to work the plan, making any adjustments necessary as you move closer and closer to your goal.

You see, the real reason why most people don't finish the race is that they simply quit running.

Persist. Keep your goal vividly in your mind and move toward it daily. Be willing to pick yourself up and learn from every mistake you make. If you get all whiney about failing along the way, the race is over for you. If you keep your determination to win and get what you want, you will win. You absolutely will win.

FATAL FLAWS OF WEAK GOALS

Let's dive right in to the bottom line first. The defining characteristics of weak goals are:

- No target
- No plan.
- No vision.

Your target is a specific goal; you must describe it to the finest detail.

Second, you must write out your plan for how you'll get what you want.

Third, you need to clearly keep your eye on the future, seeing yourself successful in your goal.

WHERE MOST GOALS GO WRONG

It's not enough to have goals. You need to be super specific about what you want. Lots of people have been saying for years that they want to be "rich and thin." And how much richer and thinner are they? Well, you know the answer to that, don't you?

Let's say that you want to go to college and get your dream job. Allow me to take you step-by-step through exactly what you'll need to do to put yourself on the fast track for getting what you want as quickly as possible.

I promise you that if you follow these steps you will succeed beyond your wildest dreams. Success is a formula. If you want something, find someone who is already doing it well, and then do exactly what she or he is doing. It works!

SEVEN SURE STEPS FOR GETTING MORE GOODIES

There are people who go through their entire lives working so very hard, yet not working smart. Success does take effort; everybody knows that. What you need to know is that when you apply the right kind of effort, you'll come up getting much more of what you want with much less work.

MINIMUM SPEED LIMIT

Let this list of steps be your guide throughout life to work smarter, not harder, to get what you want and deserve.

Minimum
Speed
Limit
45

- Set specific goals you must have.
- Plan the work.
- Hold yourself accountable.
- Stay connected with others.
- Focus on what you do want.
- Put your mind power to work.
- Recognize and use all opportunities.

1. Set specific goals you must have

Want to go to college? Take that goal one step further. Make the goal to finish college. Face it: millions of people go to school, and not as many who go will finish.

Focus on exactly what your ultimate goal is. As a goal, you'll need to state in detail when you will graduate. You can work with an advisor at school to find out what a reasonable amount of time will be to work through your program.

To make sure you stay on track as you work your way through college, keep focused on your goal. Imagine with as much deeply felt emotion as you can create how powerful and happy you will be when you achieve that goal.

In order to maintain the motivation necessary to sustain the energy to stick with a goal over the long haul, you need to generate a burning desire to have what you want.

The greater your emotion, the easier it will be for you to overcome the inevitable adversities and setbacks along the way.

EXPRESSWAY

Expressway 4.0 To move this along even faster, and make sure your mind is working in your favor to propel you to sure success and graduation in the time you allot, write your goal down and meditate on it. See the "Magic Moments" below for ideal times for doing this. Read your goal out loud, and as you do, feel the pride and satisfaction that will come with having accomplished this.

MAGIC MOMENTS IN EACH DAY IDEAL FOR PROGRAMMING YOUR MIND FOR SUCCESS

Success happens from the inside out. Once you start believing in yourself as a successful person, you'll start seeing it in the real world.

To earn your rewards in life faster, put your subconscious mind to work. There are two main times of day when your subconscious mind is especially open to your suggestions. Those are the first few minutes as you wake up, and those last few minutes right before you go to sleep.

Maximize these very special periods of time.

During these times as you drift off and first wake up, your brain waves shift to the alpha state. That's just a way of explaining the frequency of the brain wave. In the alpha state, your conscious mind is less critical and negative and your subconscious mind is more receptive to ideas.

Use these "magic moments" to focus vividly on what you want to happen. It's a great time to "reprogram your mind" for success.

2. Plan the work

Okay, so you say you have specific goals, and you have a red-hot desire to make these things happen for yourself? Great! You've mastered that first step.

Now, plan it out. That's right; get this all down in writing. And I don't want to hear that you're too spontaneous and free-spirited to take the time to do this.

You must have a plan to know exactly what you will need to do when in order to get those goodies.

Think about it: if flying by the seat of your pants and leaving success to chance worked, then there wouldn't be so many people planning and working so hard in order to reap the rewards.

Gather in close now, because this is an important secret. Ready? Okay. When it comes to getting what you want, you don't have to work as hard as you may have been led to believe.

Take control of your life and your future by knowing exactly what you want, and writing down what you need to do to make it happen.

Other people in the world who are part of the 95% or more who won't be able to support themselves upon retirement age have spent their lives working someone else's plan. You will write your own future by creating your plan based on what's important to you.

3. Hold yourself accountable

"Start each day with positive plans and end each day with a review of your accomplishments."

—Mack R. Douglas

Plan each day based on what your long and short-term goals are. Keep this plan in front of you all day, marking off each accomplishment.

At the end of the day, you have either engaged in activities that bring you closer to what you want, or you have not.

You may want to have a visual follow-up that allows you to quantify how well you did in following your plan. Some people rate themselves on a scale of 1 to 10. Others follow the A through F grading system. I keep a small notebook with me and everyday I write down between one to four actions I will take that day that will move me closer to the big goals I have.

This is NOT my "to do" list. I don't write on it every little thing I need to do. I only list the actions that move me closer to big goals. Therefore, "get the car washed" or "pick up the dry cleaning" doesn't make it into my accountability notebook.

At the end of the day, I rate myself on how well I did at accomplishing what's most important to me.

Of all the things I have done to make great things in my life happen, this tiny tool has taken me farther and ensured that I do what really matters more than any other system I have ever tried. I encourage all participants in my seminars to start similar notebooks.

4. Stay connected with others

Build lasting relationships with people. Yes, we've covered this in an earlier chapter. And it's so important to your lifelong success, you're seeing it again. Let this send a strong message to you about the importance of getting and staying connected with people. Let's review the top three compelling reasons to network:

Relationships are what matters most in life. Nothing you do, nothing, will be more important than the connections you make with family and friends.

Relationships make you smarter. Yes, it's true. You don't have to know everything, if you know who knows what you need to know, you really know quite a bit, don't you? And think about it, this principle is what makes study groups work. You can't catch every single point the professor says, but in a study group, you'll have input from people who pick up on a few points you might miss otherwise.

Relationships expand your sphere of influence. My goodness, that sounds impressive, doesn't it? All that means is that when more people know of you, your possibilities and options improve. Have you heard it's not what you know, it's who you know? Well, that works in point number 2 above. However, when it comes to going beyond your present circle, it's not who you know, it's who knows you. SO you see, the more people who know you (and, of course, like you because you're such a neat person), the more your world opens up, and with it, the more opportunities will come to you.

5. Focus on what you do want

STOP

> STOP Put an end to negative thoughts. When you find yourself focused (even obsessing) on what you don't want, immediately say, "DELETE! DELETE!" Immediately think in vivid detail about what you do want. You move toward what you think about most of the time.

We humans are such funny animals, ask anyone of us what we want, and 97% of us will start going off on what we don't want. "I don't want to be broke anymore." "I don't want to fight with my mom." "I don't want to flunk out of school." We are Johnny-on-the-spot with all that we don't want, but ask us to state what we do want and we come up speechless.

Focusing on the negative poses a big fat problem. We're all hard-wired to move towards whatever we hold in our heads. And the more emotion we attach to those thoughts, the more we're driven in that direction! Catch why this is a problem for so many people?

If you're only focused on what you don't want, even if you really, really don't want it, (especially if you really, really don't want it,) that's exactly where you're headed.

Yikes!

You've got to turn this around now by quickly getting clear about what you want and holding that in your head constantly.

Make it clear, and make your reasons for wanting it so strong that you not only think you'll get it, you know you'll get it. Keep that in the front of your mind and let go of doubt.

6. Put your mind power to work

Put daydreaming to work for you. Picture yourself several times a day achieving what you want. Make the image of you getting what you want big and bright and clear. Stay in that moment.

DETOUR

DETOUR → Take time out occasionally to ask yourself the Key Question that keeps you focused on getting more goodies: Through the day, ask yourself this:

"Does what I'm doing right now get me closer to what I want?"

If the answer is no, stop. Choose something that gets you closer to your goal. If the answer is yes, give yourself a big hug, or at least a smug smile of satisfaction, and press on with the knowledge that you're doing exactly what winners do. And you know what they call people who do what winners do, don't you? That's right. They're called winners.

Let's face up to the fact that when we start any new habit, it's possible to have temporary slips into former bad habits, right? So, as you start to go for the big time prizes in life, great relationships, prime professions, peak physical fitness, and mental health, you may find yourself off track from time to time.

Is that fair to say? Okay, it's going to happen. Not a problem, friend. Getting off course isn't the issue, getting back as soon as you realize you're trailing off is the point.

So ask yourself the Key Question in the text box above.

If you are anything like most of the people I know (including me) you are addicted to immediate gratification. You want things, and you want them now. Sound like you?

How about a great tip for helping these goals you've set come about faster? Now I will say that some achievements do take a certain amount of time, and you don't necessarily want to rush them along any faster than is reasonable. For example, most bachelor's degrees (that's most, not all) take right around four years to earn, if you can go to school full time.

Let's say you're working on something that's a bit shorter term than that. You may want to become a more confident public speaker because you know you want to be a trial lawyer. Or, you want to boost your social life and, right now, you're a bit on the shy side. These are changes that you can effect relatively quickly, if you just know the proper technique to follow.

Know how to talk to yourself and you'll get what you want a lot faster.

WHAT TO SAY WHEN YOU TALK TO YOURSELF

Affirmations are just positive things to say to yourself. It's important to take a moment to write affirmations out exactly in the way you'll be saying them. You'll want to phrase these exactly right since you'll be using these same lines again and again in order to bring about the change you want in your life.

7. Recognize and use all opportunities

First, make your affirmations start with the word "I."
Second, focus them in strictly positive language.
Third, make them specific.

SLOW DOWN

SLOW

Take the time to raise your awareness of the thoughts that constantly run through your mind.

Research shows we have words going through our minds at a rate of about 600 to 800 words a minute. Most of these words don't do much to drive us towards what we want, and in fact, often they stand in our own way by repeating negative ideas such as, "I'm terrified of speaking in front of a group" or "I'm shy about meeting people."

To deliver the results you want, make sure your affirmations are:
- Personal
- Positive
- Particular

Notice all of these follow those three parameters of being: personal, positive, and particular.

Clearly, you use "I" since you want to personalize the affirmations. They need to be positive since we know from all of the research out there that we move in the direction of our dominant thoughts and negative statements do not compute. So, in order for your subconscious to think the thought "I'm not nervous speaking in front of groups," it must first create an image of you being nervous in front of people, and then try to negate that.

As you know, those visual images have a way of sticking in our heads. They don't work because they put the negative picture solidly in your mind and that becomes your dominant thought.

Stick with what you do want.

THE SECRET FOR OVERCOMING THE BIGGEST BARRIER TO GOAL ACHIEVEMENT

Goal setting involves creating the future today, (all that creative business is very "right brain") and then creating an action plan that will ultimately take you back to the future (this planning stuff is very "left brain" logical).

The biggest barrier to goal achievement is that so many people haven't been taught that you must write down exactly what you want, and plan how you will get it.

In short, the secret to overcoming this top problem with goal setting is to use both sides of your brain.

Let those creative juices flow as you think about what you want to bring about in your life, then sit down and make a plan about how to accomplish those goals.

For example, at some time in your life, you decide you want to go to college, so you start going through the steps of researching on the web, and asking friends so you could get some idea of how to start this whole process.

As you get material in the mail, and go through all the literature, you start to form an idea of what you need to do when. You have all kinds of forms to fill out, and many different deadlines to make.

And there you have a plan.

Not all achievements in life are as seemingly well structured as applying to get into school. At least when you're doing that, someone or some institution imposes deadlines on you. Turn the paperwork in on time, or you won't be eligible for grants, loans, admittance into the college, and the list goes on and on.

However—and this is a big however—for most of the things you want in life, it will be entirely up to you to sit down and plan out exactly what you want and how you're going to get there.

For example, if you want to graduate in exactly four years and have your dream job waiting for you as soon as you walk across the stage and collect your diploma, you need to do some planning right now.

You may find that in order to get the job you want, you need to have a well-rounded experience during those four years. Your research may show that others who have moved into that job had an impressive resume that included many activities while they were in school.

So, once you have a clear idea of what you want to be doing four years from graduation, work your way backward and decide what you need to be doing during those four years so you build to the result that you want.

It's one thing to set positive goals, and another to have a burning desire to achieve them.

Now, you need to go through the critical next step of planning how you will put yourself in the position to reap the rewards you want.

Together, let's walk through how we would apply this secret to overcome the number one barrier to goal achievement.

You decide the objective of having your dream job waiting for you upon graduation is one of your long-term goals.

You picture precisely what this dream job looks like. Where are you working? In which industry? In which city do you work? How much do you travel? How formal is the environment? How big is the organization? Where could you move in the organization over the next one to ten years? What kind of hours will you hold?

Get as nitty-gritty as you like. The more details, the better.

Now, once you have firmly in your mind what you want, come back from the future and start developing a plan for this. Now it's time to move from the essential task of imagining your future in living color to the equally essential task of planning what you'll do to get there.

HOW THE LAW OF THE SLIGHT EDGE MAKES SUCCESS EASIER

You don't need to be great at everything to be truly great. With your values and goals in mind, there are really only a few key skills that you should master to be exceptional at what you do.

Master the **Six Golden Traits** of all successful people and you will be unstoppable.

YIELD

When it feels like you're living life on fast-forward, take time to step off the treadmill of life and remind yourself of these six nuggets:

6 GOLDEN TRAITS ALL SUCCESSFUL PEOPLE POSSESS
- Clear vision of what they want
- Unflinching belief in their ability to achieve their goals
- Passion to achieve
- Willingness to take daily action
- Spirit of service and contribution
- Resilience and persistence

After all that education, success comes down to this.

Of course, you are the only one who gets to define happiness for yourself. It could be material possessions, a dream job, a loving partner, or a group of fun, bright friends.

Bottom line is this: Keep it all in perspective. Hurray for you for being all you can be, striving to make the most of your talents to bring out the best in yourself.

You've heard the saying, nobody ever looked back at the end of a long life and wish they had spent more time at the office.

Balance your life. Live for results instead of regrets. Always consider the consequences for your choices and ask yourself, "Does this move me closer to what I want?" If your activity doesn't get you closer to what matters most to you, have the integrity to pass by it.

Now, go get 'em, Tiger.

Make yours an extraordinary life.

Cultivate Your "Get Along Factor"
85% of your success in life depends on your ability to get along with other people.

Get on your professor's good side from the start. Your professor can:

- Help you with material and projects you're having trouble with
- Introduce you to people in industries you'd like to work in
- Write a killer letter of recommendation

Class Etiquette

- Don't even think about missing, unless you have a really good reason, and you've mentioned this to the professor before the fact
- Come early
- Come prepared, having read the material, with a pen that writes, your book, and a notebook
- Stay awake, no matter how late you were up, and how many ounces of caffeine you need to ingest
- Stay the whole time

Snapshots from the journey

What to Know Before You Go

Before you go to see the prof during office hours, here are some tidbits that are good to know:

- Most of your teachers will appreciate if you make an appointment ahead of time, even when they have set office hours. It helps them plan their time better.

- Know exactly what you need help on. "I don't understand." Is way too general and will frustrate any instructor. You can say, "I understand up to this point, and then I get confused." Then they'll know where to start helping you.

- No fair asking for extra help just because you chose to skip class. They won't appreciate re-teaching the class. Don't wear out your welcome. Know when it's time to leave.

- Get help early. Teachers do recognize when a student is trying and they will bend over backwards to help some one who's taking responsibility for her own education.

Snapshots from the journey

Big, Bad Student Mistakes to Sidestep
Ignore these at your own peril!

These are mistakes that could:

A. Hurt your grade
B. Annoy your fellow students
C. Drive your professors crazy
D. All of the above

The answer is D. Beware these blunders:

- Not staying on top of reading assignments
- Making excuses rather than taking responsibility
- Trying to get by on charm rather than merit
- Turning assignments in late
- Asking for help too late
- Asking to make up a test

Zap the Zone Out!

No matter how smoothly you imagine you are at sneaking some shut eye in class, teachers have a sixth sense for picking up on the slightest clues that you're entering the twilight zone. Trust me on this one.

It's like when Moms can be across the country yet still know when their kids are standing in front of the open fridge "air conditioning the entire state."

Tips for staying alert when you're dangerously close to checking out the inside of your eyelids:

- Obviously, get plenty of sleep. Sleep deprivation is used as torture, you know. Get your rest.
- Drink the caffeinated beverage of your choice. Few profs care as long as you don't go sawing logs in their class.
- Sit close, it helps sustain your interest.
- Take notes with colored pencils. It keeps your brain alert and interested.
- Ask yourself, "If I were going to write a test on the material I'm hearing, what would the questions be, and what would the answers be?"

I guarantee you'll be on your toes if you give these a try.

Top Questions Never to Ask the Professor

- When is it due? (That's why they gave you the syllabus.)
- Is this testable? (Makes you sound as though you want to be spoon-fed the test and don't want to know anything beyond that.)
- I was gone last week. Did I miss anything? (Makes them think you think they don't usually say anything important. Could this have been an exception?)

Speed Read Like a Pro.

1) Move your finger over the words quickly, more quickly than you could possibly say the words in your head. Your brain prefers a brisk flow of information.

2) Put an index card over the lines you've just read to prevent the time-consuming and completely unnecessary act of backtracking. Remember, anything that's really important will be mentioned again later on, probably several times.

3) Ask questions before you read. Collect as least three key concepts with two to three supporting points each. Reading without purpose is a total waste of time.

Ready, Set, Learn!

Speed up your learning curve by being:

- Comfortable – Not reclining on the sofa, chips in one hand, remote in the other comfy, but do make sure your chair is cushy enough to support a sustained study session, your lighting is bright enough so as not to strain the eyes, and the temperature is cool enough to keep you awake.

- Confident – Look, you have a million, million brain cells. Scientists now tell us we use less than 1% of our brain power. What does this mean to you? You quite literally are a natural born genius. I guarantee you've got what it take show that class you've been dreading who's boss.

- Clear – When you sit down to study, get focused and know exactly how much material you'll be covering. As you read and review, ask yourself these questions: "What's important about this material?" and "Why is it important?" When you can answer those questions, you're ready to ace the test.

- Curious – Be inquisitive. How does this particular information fit in with what you've already learned about this topic? How would you apply the ideas and principles you're learning in "the real world"?

Snapshots
from the journey

Fun Facts to Know and Tell about Reliable Rapid Reading

- Your brain will comprehend and recall information much better if you read quickly rather than slowly enough to say the words in your head as you read.

- It's a misconception that the number of words you can read a minute is important. Far more important is the number of ideas you take in and understand from each section. Focus on lessons learned, not pages turned.

- No need to stop your flow to look up words you're unsure of as your read. Simply skip them and discover their meaning in context. You can always look them up later if you're finished reading and are completely clueless as to the meaning of the word. If it makes you crazy to hold off looking up the word, simply put a hash mark by it as you breeze by it and look it up later.

Snapshots from the journey

Not All Requisites are Really Required

You may be able to escape that killer class after all. Questions to ask your academic advisor to discover if there's an easier way than to take a class that will sink your GPA:

- Is there a suitable substitute I can take instead? (You never know, these rules change all the time. Your advisor will have the latest 411 on this.)

- Can I audit it first? (And if so, can you do it for no cost to you?)
- Can I take it in the summer? (When other classes won't be competing for your attention.)
- If there is absolutely no alternative but to take this class, who is the best teacher who teaches it? And by "best" I mean, of course, easiest.

Syllabi (That's plural for Syllabus)
Your Golden Ticket to an "A"

This critical document tells you everything you need to:

- Be well-prepared for class.
- Know what's due when (Remember, it's the kiss of death to ask the prof when anything is due. Your teachers aren't your parents and they don't want you acting like kids.).

- Know how much assignments and tests (and being prepared for class) count toward your final grade.
- Find your professor (office hours, office times, phone number) as soon as you find out you need a hand.

Snapshots from the journey

Less is More

Brilliant though your professor may be, not every word he utters is noteworthy. He knows this.

Learn how to Mind Map® your notes. See the book "Using Both Sides of Your Brain" or "The Mind Map Book" both by Tony Buzan, the genius who created Mind Mapping®.

You'll discover how easy and fun it is to play to your brain's

natural strengths as you learn just how quickly you can capture key concepts and commit them to memory.

You'll find yourself taking far fewer notes yet remembering much more. You can easily test yourself to see how much you recall by rewriting your Mind Map® from memory. It's a thrill to begin to appreciate how very quickly you can learn new material, at a fraction of the effort you were putting forth before.

The Ideal Time to Study

1. When you prepare for class. Reading before class, even a speed read, prepares your mind to comprehend, retain, and recall the lecture material better.

2. Five to ten minutes after you've heard the lecture material, your memory will actually get a bit better as you synthesize the new material with what you knew before class. This makes those few minutes after class ideal times to review your

Mind Map®.

3. Twenty-four hours later. Even if it's not convenient at that time to pull out your notes to review, simply mentally reconstruct your map and you'll find yourself recalling more and more material with very little effort.

4. One week later, before looking at your notes, redo your map. When you've written down as much as you can recall, look at the map and fill in any blanks.

5. One month later, again, recreate that map. Make sure you do this, you're sure to need this material again at test time!

Snapshots
from the journey

Don't Study!

Do not even think of wasting your valuable time studying what you already know. It's amazing how many people will literally spend time reviewing concepts they could recite in their sleep.

Why?

Probably because it's an ego boost, and helps us feel as though we really know quite a bit.

It's also easy to be lulled into a false sense of security because you've got the answers right there.

It's a time drain. Move on.

There's an exception, though. It's helpful before you learn any new material to spend about five minutes reviewing what you do know about the topic.

Because our memory works by connecting new material to the concepts we already hold in our head, you'll find comprehension and recall much easier when you have those five minutes to review what you already know about the topic at hand.

Set the Stage for Easy Learning.

Just like Pavlov trained pooches to salivate at the sound of a bell, you can prepare yourself to learn quickly by following the same steps every time you study.

You can anchor yourself to learning the same way Pavlov anchored the dogs to salivate when he rang the bell and provided dinner. You'll recall that after pairing these three actions, soon, he no longer had to provide dinner. The dogs would salivate just because the bell rang.

Here's how you can use that fun little study to your benefit.

Every time you go to study, make the same preparation.

For example, first, pick just a few places you enjoy studying.

Now, each time you go there to study, go through the same ritual. You can bring out your favorite pen, for example, your notebook, paper clips, and sticky notes. If you like to drink (and we're talking non-alcoholic, please), you can have the same thing from the same cup.

As you prepare your workspace, your mind has anchored this ritual to learning. So, you are more likely to be mentally prepared to take in new info if you consistently have the same preparation ritual each time you study.

Cool, isn't it?

Recognize Gifts of Time

It seems as we get older, the more of our time goes to taking care of others and all of our obligations.

Doesn't it drive you crazy to wait? Well, instead of allowing yourself to slowly be driven up a wall by all that wasted time, put that to work for you.

Make up several 3x5 cards with study points from each of your classes. Carry these cards with you wherever you go. Have them when you're waiting for your daughter to finish her soccer game, or when you're standing in line at the bank, or when you're sitting in traffic.

Get creative and not only will you be learning a lot, you'll not even notice those annoying waiting games.

TV as Time Vampire

Ok, I confess, I really like my TV. I'm not here to tell you not to watch. It can be fun, it's certainly cheap, and you can even watch some shows with your kids. What's not to like?

Well, research now shows us that our TVs are on in excess of seven hours a day. Yes, you read that right. Seven hours a day is the average American households have their TVs on.

Here's what we know about those pesky hummers. Even if you're not actually watching the tube, even if you're just studying in the same room where the TV is on, it will distract you.

What this means is that although you may think you're studying for two hours, the amount of time you're mind is focused on the subject you're supposedly studying is tremendously reduced.

You're much better off leaving the room, having 30 minutes of concentrated study, and then coming back and enjoying a show.

Snapshots from the journey

Jump-start Your Job Search

Doesn't matter what year you are in school, begin your job search right now.

Most college students make the fatal error of waiting six weeks before graduation and then sending out 200 unsolicited resumes within a 100 mile radius of the college. Imagine what it must be like for all those organizations on the receiving end of all those resumes!

You don't want to be putting your resume out there at the same time everyone in your graduating class is flooding the market with theirs.

Review this chapter and make a plan to start your job search now. Begin with networking, looking into interning and move on to booking information interviews.

Snapshots from the journey

Things to Put on Your Resume.

Include more than your grades. Companies need people who can:

- Speak well
- Problem solve
- Work in teams
- And Write well

Make sure you include evidence that you can do all of these.

Other items to include in your resume:
- Clubs
- Summer programs
- Leadership positions
- Internships
- Study abroad

Be special and stand out.

When you have informational interviews, ask the person you're interviewing what were the most interesting items they've seen on resumes lately.

Keys to Networking

You've heard "It's not what you know, it's who you know." True in part. However, sometimes "It's not who you know, it's who knows you."

Everyone talks about networking, few people get it.

Remember the following:

- Ask yourself first, "What can I do for this person?"

- Business etiquette is critical. After you've talked with the other person, and decided that there is a connection between you, ask, "Could we exchange cards? I'd like to stay in touch." Don't just pass yours out like after-dinner mints.

- Once you receive their card, comment on it. You can say something about the color choices, or ask how they chose the name, or how long they've been with that company. Just make a point of obviously reading the card. So many people just shove the cards in their pocket or bags.

- Be sure to stay in touch. You can do this via snail mail, or even e-mail.

- Dropping a line once every six to 12 weeks is fine.

People Love to Help!

Let them help you. Your professors are in general extremely well-connected and they know many people who are in the very industry you're interested in finding more about.

Ask your professor, "Who do you know who would be willing to talk with me more about how they got into this industry?"

You might be amazed at how willing people are to tell you all about how they got started in their jobs.

Getting those informational interviews is key to getting your foot in the door.

Just make sure you are gracious and that you send a thank you note after the interview. Also, let the prof who connected you know how the interview went. They enjoy helping and knowing how you did.

Leadership Potential

Can you prove you've got it? So few have proof.

The highest paid skill is oral communication. More specifically, it's the ability to inspire others to be who they are at their best.

Show you've done that.

And what's the best way to go about that? Simple, join clubs you'd enjoy and work up to a leadership position.

Make sure you keep a log of what you've done in those volunteer positions. This includes making note of any compliments you get from others. When you hear one, be sure to ask, "May I quote you on that?" They will be flattered, trust me, and you will have a great testimonial.

Balance is Key in All You Do

In the book, "The Power of Full Engagement" the authors make the compelling argument that energy, not time is our most valuable resource.

College can be one of the most fun and rewarding times of your life. Take time to enjoy the journey. Stop and smell the roses. Make friends. Make memories.

You'll always be glad you did.

Be Specific About Your Goals

Remember Lily Tomlin's line:

"All my life I wanted to be somebody. Now I see I should have been more specific."

Be clear about what you want and state your goals in specific terms. This will focus your energy and attention and allow you to accomplish much more, much faster. This is because you won't be spinning your wheels with unnecessary activities.

Make sure you have plans that detail what you'll do to get your goals.

And finally, hold yourself accountable. Literally write down at the beginning of every day what you will accomplish, and at the end of the day, record how well you followed through on your plans.

This simple act alone will put you head and shoulders above most people who haven't a clear clue where they are now and where they are headed.

Use the "Magic Moments" in the Day to Elevate Your Self-Image

Psychologists have said for ages that we'll never rise above our image of ourselves.

So, if you doubt your ability to finish your degree on time, get the job of your dreams, or earn the income you desire, you're putting unnecessary restrictions on yourself.

Begin using declarations which state in a positive, personal, powerful way that you are the kind of person to achieve everything you desire.

Also include in these declarations the necessary actions to move you forward in your goals.

Right before you fall asleep and right as you wake up are ideal times to recite these declarations. This is because the conscious mind, which is most likely to resist these exciting ideas, is quiet.

So, use these "magic moments" to recite your declarations. They will be the last thing you hear and the first thing on your mind.

116 © Crystal Jonas

Keep Score!

You should always know where you stand in relation to your goals.

Are you getting a bit closer every day? Are you moving forward more quickly on some days rather than others? Do yourself a favor and look closely at what you might be doing to accelerate your success.

Even if your accountability system is one of those tiny spiral notebooks, this is fine.

You'll want to know what your goals and plans are each day, and then write down what you will do to move you closer to your goals.

The accountability notebook will naturally enhance your focus and increase how easy it is for you to "tune in to opportunity" because you will have "TOMA" of your plans. (TOMA stands for top of mind awareness.)

Since we get what we focus on, this little process will yield big results in giving you laser-guided focus.

About the Author

Like you, Crystal Jonas had a dream to make it through college on schedule without keeping her nose in a book the whole time. Using the tips, tools, and techniques she presents here, she not only graduated, she had a blast in the process and ended up with a great career upon graduation.

After receiving her B.A. in Communications, Crystal became an Air Force officer and went on to serve as an Assistant Professor of English at the U.S. Air Force Academy. While she was there, she helped design and deliver a course on accelerated learning techniques that help college students learn and retain more with less effort.

Now the owner of her own consulting and seminar company, Tap Your Genius, Inc., Crystal travels the country teaching students about happiness and high performance.

Crystal is recognized by schools, associations, and organizations for her audience-centered programs that are fun, energetic, relevant, and memorable.

To book Crystal at your school or conference, contact:

Crystal Jonas
Manitou Springs, CO
719.291.0366
or e-mail: Crystal@CrystalJonas.com

KEYNOTES AND SEMINARS FOR COLLEGE STUDENTS OF ALL AGES

College Programs for:
- Orientation
- College-bound Students
- Nontraditional Students
- Outreach
- Student Athletes
- At-risk Students
- Greek-sponsored Functions

- Student Leadership (SGA)
- Commencement
- Career Days and Job Fairs
- Summer Events
- Club and Association Events
- TRIO Programs

BENEFITS
- Recruit students
- Retain them
- Help them secure meaningful jobs after graduation

College students of all ages will benefit from these fun, motivational, and memorable programs designed just for them.

- "Succeeding in College Academics: What Professors Won't Tell You and Your Friends Don't Know"
- "Living an Extraordinary Life"
- "Fitting in Fast: How to Adjust Quickly and Have a Great Social Life in College"
- "The Power of Integrity And Vision: How to Create and Lead High Performance Teams"
- "Balancing Life and School: Nontraditional Solutions for Nontraditional Students"
- "Athletes Acing Academics" One of a Kind Program Plays to Student Athletes' Strengths

To Book Crystal at your school or conference:
Crystal Jonas
Crystal@CrystalJonas.com
719-291-0366

INDEX

A

"A" 3, 31, 40, 102
   Document that guides you to
   an "A" 40
Abroad 69, 70, 110
   Study abroad 110
   Benefits of studying abroad 69,
   70
Academic advancement 13
Accelerated Learning 22, 49, 118
Accountable 82, 84, 86, 115
   Hold self accountable 82
Active listening 6, 10
Advancement 13, 63
Answers 3, 6, 22, 31, 32, 74,
   97, 105
   Key times answers are given
   away 2, 31, 32
   Test answers given 3, 31, 32
Apply 26, 27, 71, 84, 92, 99
Appointment 4, 5, 8, 15, 16,
   65, 95
Ask for what you want 74
Asking for help 16, 65, 96
Assignments 16, 17, 40, 42, 96,
   102
Assignments, late 16, 96
Associations 9, 56, 69, 75, 118

B

Backtracking 27, 98
   Speed bump to speed reading
   26, 27, 28
Books v, 17, 23, 27, 28, 32, 50,
   53, 62

Free v
Brain 12, 17, 22, 23, 24, 25, 27, 28,
   37, 46, 47, 48, 49, 50, 53,
   55, 56, 83, 85, 86, 91, 97, 98,
   99, 100, 103
   Brain power 53, 55
Breathe deeply 50
Business people 65, 82

C

Caffeine 18, 22, 94
Career iv, v, vii, 3, 8, 16, 17, 61,
   62, 63, 64, 65, 71, 74, 75, 76,
   78, 79, 118
Class 1, 2, 3, 4, 5, 6, 7, 8, 9, 10,
   11, 12, 13, 14, 15, 16, 17, 18,
   19,22, 23, 24, 30, 31, 32, 33,
   34, 35, 36, 37, 38, 39, 40, 41,
   42, 43, 46, 47, 48, 49, 55, 57,
   58, 64, 66, 94, 95, 97, 101,
   102, 104, 109
   Go early 4, 29
   Leave early 4
   Participation 1, 5
   Reasons to go to class 2
   Skipping class 2, 3, 18, 33, 66
   Stand out in a crowd 5, 41,
   110
Clear 5, 14, 15, 22, 23, 24, 26, 28,
   30, 60, 64, 78, 79, 82, 88, 89,
   92, 93, 99, 115
Clues 21, 25, 26, 29, 97
Comfortable 6, 22, 23, 36, 39, 65,
   99
   Comfortable vs. casual 22

INDEX

Comprehension 30, 32, 105
    When reading 29
    Relaxed comprehension 22
Confident 23, 24, 42, 56, 89, 99
Core 14, 37
    Core requirements 37
Curious 23, 24, 99

D

Detour 18, 33, 89
Discretionary 10% 5
Divide and conquer 34, 39
Dream job iv, 1, 8, 61, 62,
    69, 84, 92, 93

E

Effort iv, v, 21, 26, 39, 64,
    79, 84, 103, 104, 118
    Less effort 21, 26
Excellence 78
Exercise 32, 51, 55, 56, 79
    Exercise your brain 56
Expressway 5, 27, 39, 83, 85
Extra credit 1, 6

F

Falling Rocks 4, 24, 38
Flow 50, 91, 98, 100
Focus 3, 5, 6, 24, 25, 28, 29, 30,
    53, 59, 60, 62, 63, 78, 79, 82,
    84, 85, 86, 88, 90, 100, 115,
    117
    Greater focus 29
    On demand 53, 59
    When reading 22

G

Goal 24, 28, 37, 39, 51, 81, 82,
    83, 84, 85, 89, 91, 92
Goals vi, 24, 28, 39, 40, 51, 63, 79,
    81, 82, 83, 84, 85, 86, 87, 89,
    91, 92,
    Goal achievement 81, 91, 92
    Set specific goal 82, 84-86, 89
    Weak goal 84
GPA 35, 68, 101
Grades v, 3, 8, 9, 16, 17, 21, 32,
    36, 37, 42, 51, 62, 110
    Discretionary 10% 3
    Better grades v, 21, 42
Grading criteria 40, 42
Great Job 64, 65

H

Help iv, vii, 1, 5, 8, 13, 15, 16, 17,
    24, 25, 26, 28, 29, 30, 34, 36,
    36, 37, 39, 41, 46, 55, 64, 65,
    66, 67, 77, 94, 95, 96, 112,
    118, 119
    Asking for help 15, 65, 96
    Asking for help too late 96
Highlight 40
    What to highlight 40
    Syllabus items to highlight 40
Homework 22, 25, 35

I

Imagine 10, 15, 35, 36, 43, 47, 50,
    51, 64, 85, 109
Index cards 58
Influence 5, 9, 59, 87

INDEX

Expand your sphere of influence 87

Initiative 14, 15, 70, 76, 77, 79

Interviews iv, 73, 74, 76, 109, 110, 112
  No pressure interviews 110, 112
  High visibility interviews 74
  Informational interviews 110, 112

J

Job iv, 1, 8, 9, 13, 14, 36, 46, 60, 61, 62, 63, 64, 65, 68, 69, 70, 71, 73, 74, 76, 77, 78, 84, 92, 93, 109, 116
  Dream job iv, vi, 1, 7, 52, 61, 62, 69, 84, 92, 93
  Great Job 64, 65
  Job search 61, 63, 69, 71, 109
  Job search tools 71
  Ideal time to begin job search 61, 63, 64

K

Key concepts 5, 9, 10, 24, 25, 26, 29, 38, 43, 46, 59, 98, 103
Key skills 77, 78, 79, 92
Key terms 9, 10
Key words 10, 22, 46

L

Leadership v, 63, 69, 70, 76, 77, 79, 110, 113
  Leadership potential 76, 79,

113
Learning v, 3, 5, 9, 13, 21, 22, 24, 40, 45, 48, 49, 54, 56, 65, 99, 106, 107, 118
  Accelerated Learning 22, 49, 118
  Easier Learning 21, 26
Leave early 4, 14, 15
Listening 6, 10, 49, 66, 70, 75
  Active listening 6, 10
Living an Extraordinary Life v, 119

M

Memory 9, 13, 21, 25, 26, 29, 33, 38, 45, 46, 48, 49, 55, 56, 71, 103, 104, 105
  Overview 9
Mentor 64, 65, 66, 67
Mind Mapping® 12, 103
Mind Maps® 12
Mind Power 24, 84, 88
Minimum Speed Limit 2, 57, 67, 77, 84
Mistakes 11, 15, 65, 79, 96
  Biggest mistakes students make 11, 15
Music 45, 48, 49
Myths 21, 29
  Reading myths 21, 20

N

Network 66, 67, 71, 75, 76, 87
Networking 61, 64, 67, 68, 70, 75, 109, 111
Note taking 6, 12
  Shorthand 9, 43

INDEX

Notes 2, 5, 9, 10, 12, 15, 18, 19, 22, 23, 36, 37, 38, 43, 46, 48, 59, 66, 67, 69, 75, 97, 103, 104, 106
   Brief and memorable 9, 69
   Well-chosen 18, 69
Noteworthy 31, 43, 103
NTs 53, 54, 55
   Nontraditional students v, 53, 54, 58, 119

O

Oasis 6, 47, 78, 82
Office hours 8, 16, 40, 41, 95, 102
   By appointment 16, 40
   Popping in 16
Opportunities 53, 56, 62, 63, 65, 68, 69, 84, 88, 90
   To pull ahead 53, 56, 71
Overload 46
   Information overload 46

P

Paper 5, 22, 31, 42, 51, 59, 106
Participation 1, 6
   Participation in class 6
Pass 13, 15, 31, 34, 35, 37, 40, 80, 93, 111
   How to Pass a killer class 34-40
Prerequisite 34, 36
Preview 23, 34, 37
Professional Organizations 63
Professors i, iv, v, 1, 5, 6, 7, 8, 9, 11, 13, 14, 15, 16, 17, 18, 33, 37, 39, 40, 41, 64, 65, 96, 112, 119
   Professor's good side 4, 94
   What Professors want 13
   What never to admit to professors 15
Promoted iv, 54, 73, 76
   Qualities of people who get promoted quickly 73, 76

Q

Quantum Learning 49
Questions 4, 6, 7, 8, 11, 12, 13, 14, 15, 19, 22, 24, 28, 29, 30, 66, 75, 97, 98, 99, 101
   Stupid questions 6
   Three questions never to ask 11, 13, 98
   Questions you may want to ask 22, 75
Quit 45, 49, 83

R

Read 3, 6, 7, 9, 12, 13, 15, 18, 22, 23, 24, 25, 27, 28, 29, 30, 32, 37, 38, 40, 41, 42, 46, 48, 56, 57, 85, 94, 98, 99, 100, 104, 108
Reading 10, 15, 17, 18, 21, 22, 23, 24, 25, 26, 27, 28, 29, 30, 37, 58, 96, 98, 100, 104, 111
   Backtracking 26, 27, 98
   Clues 21, 24, 25, 28, 97
   Myths 21, 29
   Speed reading 24, 25
   Sub-vocalizing 26, 27, 29

INDEX

Reading without purpose 28, 98

Reasons to go to class 3

Recall 9, 22, 24, 25, 26, 27, 30, 43, 46, 48, 50, 51, 55, 58, 100, 103, 104, 105, 106

Goals of reading 26

Recommendations 64

Letters of recommendation 8, 71

Relationships 64, 67, 70, 87, 89

Building lasting relationships 64, 67, 70, 87, 89

Remembering 27, 38, 103

Key terms 9, 10

Rest Area 51

Resumes 61, 63, 64, 68, 75, 109, 110

Resumes that attract job offers 64, 68

Review ii, 6, 9, 10, 15, 26, 29, 34, 35, 36, 37, 46, 57, 59, 68, 86, 87, 99, 104, 105, 109

Ritual 48, 49, 106

Rush Hour 23, 34

S

Scenic Route 62

Seminars iv, v, 87, 119

Shorthand 10, 43

Skipping class 4, 18, 33

Slow 14, 25, 29, 90

Speed Bump 26, 27, 28

Speed reading 24, 25

State dependent learning 48

Stop 12, 23, 27, 41, 43, 75, 79, 88, 89, 100, 114

Study abroad 110

Study groups 87

Divide and conquer 34, 39

Study less 45, 46

Studying abroad 69, 70

Subconscious 48, 85, 86, 91

Sub-vocalizing 26, 28

Success i, v, 1, 2, 4, 33, 51, 54, 62, 73, 77, 80, 81, 82, 83, 84, 85, 86, 87, 92, 93, 94, 117

Professional success v

Where success starts 81, 82

Summer 34, 35, 36, 69, 101, 110

Syllabus 13, 15, 24, 33, 37, 39, 40, 98, 102

Academic advancement 13

T

Talent 73, 76

Talent companies hire for 73, 76

Teacher's assistant 8

Terms 9, 10, 115

Test 3, 4, 13, 14, 16, 22, 25, 26, 31, 32, 34, 35, 48, 51, 58, 96, 97, 98, 99, 103, 104

Testable 5, 12, 13, 33, 98

"Is this testable?" 12, 98

Thank you note 66, 69, 112

Time iv, vii, 2, 4, 5, 6, 7, 8, 9, 10, 13, 14, 15, 16, 17, 18, 23, 24, 25, 28, 30, 32, 33, 34, 35, 36,

INDEX

37, 39, 41, 42, 46, 48, 49, 50,
51, 54, 56, 57, 58, 59, 60, 63,
64, 65, 66, 69, 70, 71, 74, 75,
76, 77, 78, 79, 80, 82, 85, 86,
88, 89, 90, 93, 94, 95, 98, 101,
104, 105, 106, 107, 108, 109,
114, 116, 118
    Control time of killer class 31,
        34, 36, 101

U

Understand 9, 17, 24, 25, 26, 37,
    39, 43, 55, 76, 95, 100
    Understand goals of reading 24

V

Voice mail 41
    Be sure to leave voice mail 41

W

Well-defined schedule 60
Write 5, 7, 9, 10, 12, 17, 31, 38,
    42, 43, 57, 58, 67, 69, 70, 82,
    83, 85, 86, 87, 90, 91, 94, 97,
    110, 115, 117

Y

Yield 16, 25, 79, 93, 117

Z

Zone out 13, 37, 97
    Keep from zoning out in class
        11, 18

Start Here for College and Career Success

Success is a snap when you know the shortcuts.

Concerned about college? Many who start don't finish. Imagine how fun, simple and rewarding college will be when you have this easy to follow, step-by-step guide clearly showing you the way to graduation and your dream job.

Finally! The answers are here!

Discover:

- What not to study so you'll save tons of time!
- How your professors can help you land your dream job
- 12 imaginative ways to pass a killer class
- Nontraditional solutions for nontraditional students
- Opportunities to pull ahead

Crystal Jonas cracks the code. A former instructor and academic advisor at the USAF Academy, one of the nation's most academically demanding schools reveals the secrets to college success.

- 8 of the biggest mistakes students make
- How to avoid your professors' pet peeves
- Winning ways to study smarter, not harder
- Powerful plan to launch your career while in school

Who should read this book:
- College Students
- Adults returning to school
- College athletes
- College-bound Students
- Students with scholarships
- International students
- Anyone who wants to get that diploma and enjoy the experience!

Crystal Jonas, is an award winning speaker and eight-time published author. She writes about happiness and high performance and has help thousands of people unlock their potential to succeed in school and work.

To ask about scheduling Crystal Jonas for a keynote, workshop or seminar for students, faculty or staff development, email: Crystal@CrystalJonas.com. You can also call or text 719.291.0366.

CRYSTAL JONAS

This popular guide on college success has shown thousands of people the faster, surer way to reach their educational goals. It can help you too.

www.ingramcontent.com/pod-product-compliance
Lightning Source LLC
LaVergne TN
LVHW061218060426
835508LV00014B/1345